LIBRARY OF CONGRESS CATALOG CARD NUMBER: 75-24948

Production supervised by
The Book Studio Inc.

Dedicated to

Norman and Molly Rockwell

and

THE CURTIS
PUBLISHING COMPANY

FOUR S PRODUCTIONS INC.

Dr. Donald R. Stoltz ....President
Donald J. Klein, Esq. ....Vice President
Marshall L. Stoltz ....Secretary-Treasurer

Board of Directors

Donald E. Artzt, Esq.   Bob Grosnoff   Louis A. Cinquanto, Sr.

CONTENTS

NORMAN ROCKWELL

Norman Rockwell
This set of books is a tribute, a tribute to a man whose face is familiar to many of us, whose name is known by most of us and whose creations are a part of all of us.

It is a show of appreciation to a man who is as American as Uncle Sam, as devoted as the Boy Scouts and as talented as the masters of the Renaissance.

It is a salute to one of America's most beloved men—Norman Rockwell—artist, illustrator and historian.

These books contain all the covers that Mr. Rockwell painted for *The Saturday Evening Post*. It is the first time that a complete, full-size, full-color collection of Norman Rockwell's *Post* covers has been assembled and made available to all collectors. The covers are a truly remarkable history. They are a storybook of our country, encompassing over sixty years of everyday happenings, a living, vibrant, unvarnished documentation of America.

In 1943 a fire in Norman Rockwell's studio in East Arlington, Vermont destroyed many of his original canvases, memorabilia and *Saturday Evening Post* covers. In 1969, "*The Post*" temporarily ceased production (it was reorganized in 1971 and continues today to be published monthly), and many of its archives were lost or removed. Copies of these magazines and covers are now as rare as the original oils from which they were reproduced.

To be able to accumulate, categorize, restore, edit and reproduce these covers in a fashion as close as possible to the original covers is a labor of love, and a special note of appreciation must go to Mr. Donald Artzt, Mr. Bob Grosnoff, Mr. Louis Cinquanto, and Mr. Donald Klein whose time, effort, knowledge, and perseverance have been invaluable to us. We also thank Mrs. Iris Wallach, Assistant Curator of the Norman Rockwell Museum in Philadelphia, Miss Donna Mayer, and Mrs. Betty Wilson for their assistance. In addition, we are deeply grateful to Mr. William Gardiner and Mr. Starkey Flythe, Jr. of *The Saturday Evening Post* and to the Old Corner House of Stockbridge, Massachusetts, where many Rockwell treasures are permanently displayed for the public to enjoy. For their support and encouragement our gratitude is extended to C. Richard Spiegel, President of River Shore, Ltd., and Arch Patterson, Vice-President of River Shore, Ltd. and President of the Rockwell Society. Finally, we express appreciation to Michael Fine for his role in bringing this project to realization.

In 1972 Bernard Danenberg Art Galleries of New York compiled an exhibit of *Post* covers, as well as original Rockwell oils and drawings, and toured the country with this collection, generating monumental interest and adding millions of new Rockwell fans to the rolls. Throngs of younger generation admirers revealed the agelessness of these artistic treasures. People hurried to their attics and basements to search for old *Post* magazines so that the covers could be preserved and enjoyed.

It was as a result of this exhibit and the massive interest of those seeing it, as well as an appeal from serious Rockwell collectors, that we decided to reproduce the original covers in three volumes, exactly as they appeared in print, thus preserving for future generations the art and illustration of this gifted American.

Seeing and reading these volumes is more than a moment's entertainment; to watch the sheer enjoyment of people getting to know Rockwell is to understand what our books are all about.

"People love studying other people." That says it all, and we hope that the pages which follow provide such a medium of love and insight to all who open these books.

Dr. Donald R. Stoltz, President
Marshall L. Stoltz, Curator
Norman Rockwell Museum
Philadelphia, Pennsylvania

"Wartime Thanksgiving"

It's 1943. Thanskgiving. Although it should be a happy day for all, it is only bittersweet; the war is raging and our fathers, sons, and husbands are off fighting the enemy in all corners of the world.

At this time, Norman Rockwell feels that he has to put aside his thoughts of puppy dogs and freckled-faced kids, and instead lend his attention to what may be referred to as a dismal side of life. And yet, as Rockwell portrays in this somewhat darkened picture, a light of love and comfort shows through the gloom. We see in this Thanksgiving cover a young girl in war-torn Italy draped in the warm coat of a passing G. I. We see also that she is about to share the meager rations from his G. I. mess kit. Still, no matter how meager the rations, how temporary the warmth, or how fleeting the charity, she is taking the opportunity to stop and offer grace to the Almighty for what she has been blessed with.

Rockwell's message comes through loud and clear: Remember, Americans, on this Thanksgiving Day there are millions of others around the world less fortunate than we. And in our haste, let us give thanks for what we have, and offer up a prayer of hope for those who have not. Once again, we see the magnificence of Rockwell's artistry as he captures all too well the devastated and crumpled ruins of Europe's age-old buildings, and the hope that one day they, together with her people, may once again stand proud.

THE SATURDAY EVENING
POST
NOVEMBER 27, 1943
10¢
BILLION-DOLLAR PLANE BUILDER
By ALVA JOHNSTON
A Gay Short Story
By ROBERT CARSON
U.S.
Norman Rockwell
THANKSGIVING

"New Year's Eve"

It is New Year's Eve and the Magic Hour. Twelve o'clock midnight is the time for celebrating, ringing bells, blowing horns, and for most people, noisily ushering in the New Year. But the young lady in this picture has set herself apart from the merriment of the crowds. Her boyfriend (once again, Willie Gillis) is off fighting the war. So, the only place for her to be on this night is home, snug in bed, with a newly arrived letter.

But she's not really alone. As we see, Willie is keeping a close watch on his "Hometown Honey" from his threefold vantage point overlooking her bed. He has seen her read and reread every word before quietly dozing off to sleep. And while this letter will soon join the rest of her collection, it now prompts her to dream of Willie so very many miles away.

In a most difficult artistic achievement, Rockwell has once again incorporated the use of black-and-white photos in an oil painting. He has also used his talents to capture realistically the various textures of cloth. Notice, for example, the pink satin bathrobe thrown casually across the bed and the matching pink slippers with carnation.

While Rockwell was making the colored sketch of the young woman, he noticed a problem which caused him a bit of embarrassment. As he began to sketch he became aware of two strangely large humps in the covers over the girl's chest. He said, "Betty, take your hands off your chest. They're making humps in the covers." "Those aren't my hands, Mr. Rockwell," said Betty, blushing deeply. "Oh," Rockwell quietly said.

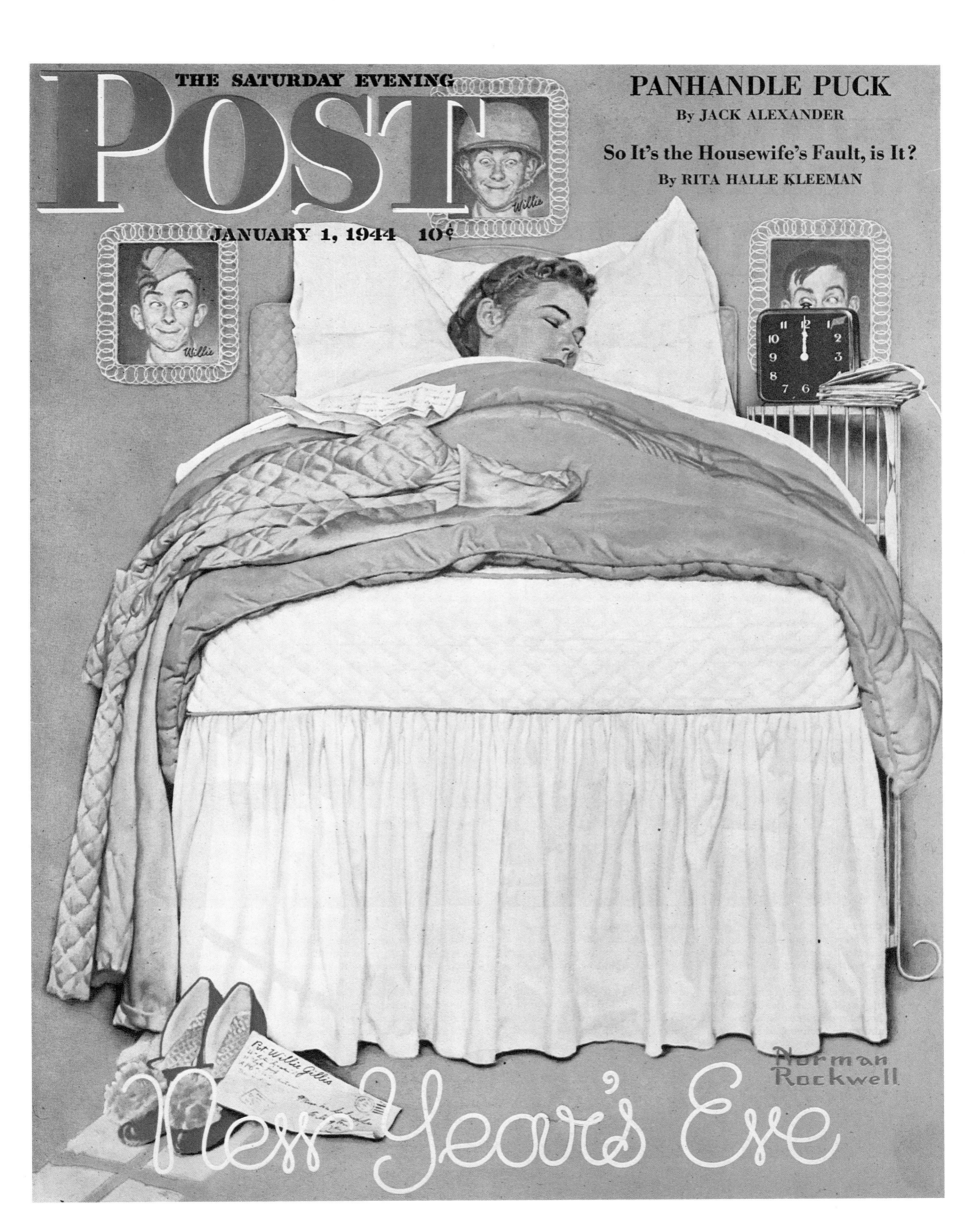

"Tattoo Artist"

In this cover, the sailor, having just pulled into port, has already acquired a new girl friend, Betty. Considering the list of names visible on his arm, it is plain to see that he has already visited numerous ports throughout the world. His conquests are many, much to the delight of the local tattoo artist, whom he keeps quite busy.

Both sailor and artist are posed against a backdrop of the tattooist's sample sheet. Notice that the tattoos being offered are shown in the same color density as they would appear on the skin. We also see that the old salt is quite a meticulous fellow. The hair comb is held in place by a pack of cigarettes in his pocket. As we glance upward, however, we see the gentleman's less-than-abundant hair, and we wonder why he needs the comb at all. We also have to chuckle at the color-coordinated clothes of the tattoo artist, for his shirt and socks seem to have come from the same bolt of cloth.

True to his total attention to detail, Rockwell has captured the weatherbeaten complexion of the sailor. Just below the confidently perched cap, and especially below the ears, various shades of sunburned-turned-tanned skin are visible.

The tattoo artist cover, Rockwell maintained, was very well received, as were most of those he did bearing on the war. The model for the tattooist in this picture was his good friend and fellow *Post* illustrator Mead Schaeffer. Schaeffer claimed that Rockwell painted his posterior larger that it really was; Rockwell claimed that he didn't. Judging from this picture, it is evident that the argument was never really settled.

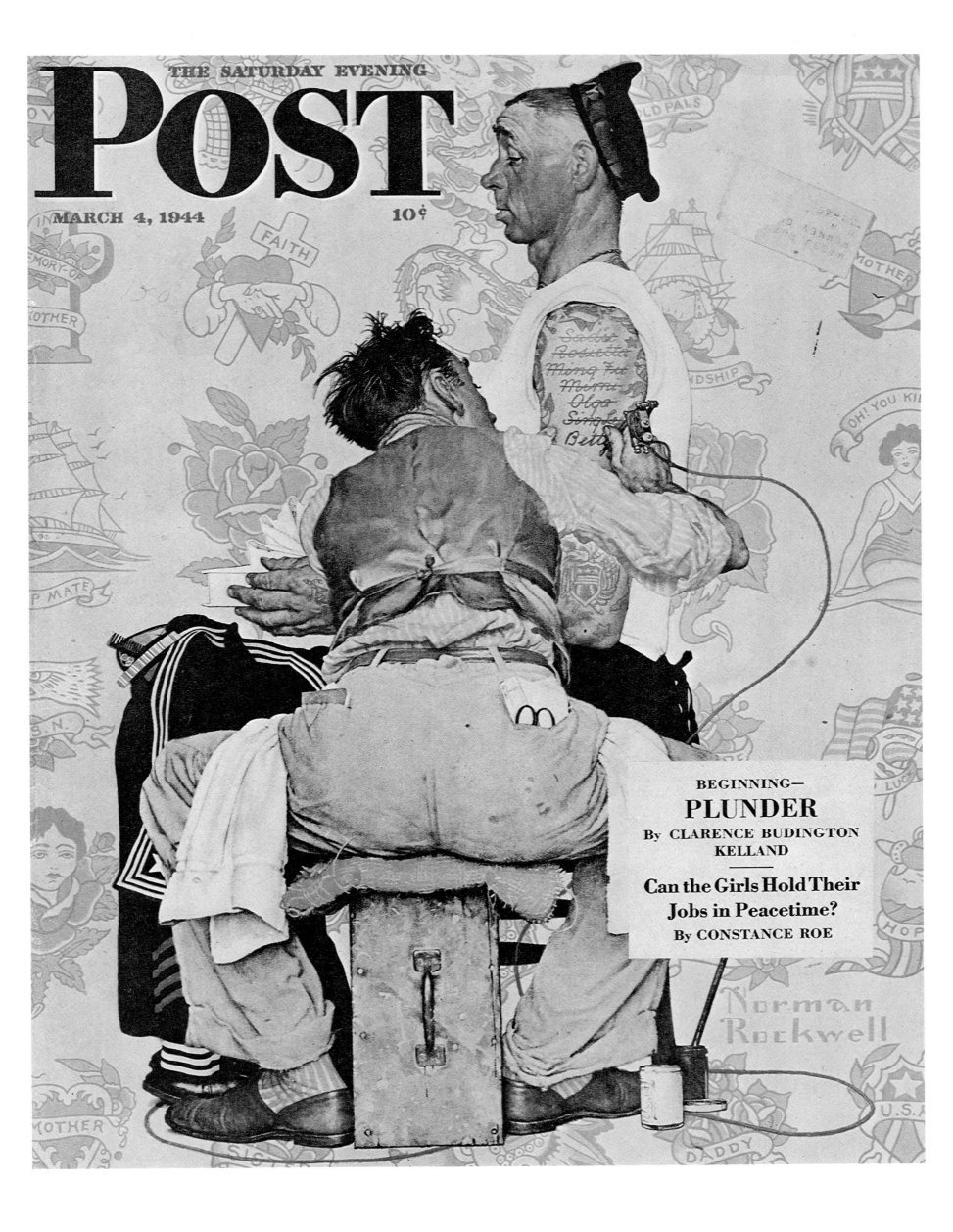

"The Armchair General"

Despite the times, this cover shows a definite note of optimism. As the war rages on, this father of three servicemen stays closely tuned in to his radio. Monitoring the war's developments, he carefully pencils in each advance and each retreat with the deftness of a battlefield general. The square-set jaw and tightly clenched cigar show the air of determination not only of this armchair general but of Americans the world over.

Once again, Rockwell shows his flair for detail. Notice the small photos of the armchair general's sons. Each is in a different branch of the service. The white banner with the red border and three blue stars indicates that, as of now, all is well with the boys. Perhaps one may recall that when one of those blue stars turned to gold, it meant that a serviceman would no longer be returning home. Notice also the black-and-white photos of Generals Douglas MacArthur and Dwight David Eisenhower looking down on the father, almost saying with resolve, "Don't worry. We'll get your boys home and win this thing yet." Other details which stand out in this picture are the old-fashioned radio, the map on the wall (showing details of European areas), the wallpaper, the exactness of the chair in which the father is sitting, and the cats on the rug.

THE SATURDAY EVENING
POST

APRIL 29, 1944   10¢

A HILARIOUS NEW SERIAL
By PHIL STONG

SLICKEST TRICK OF THE WAR
By LT. (j.g.) WILLIAM BRADFORD HUIE

Norman Rockwell

ARMCHAIR GENERAL

"The Fireman"

One day in the early forties, while rummaging through an old junk shop, Rockwell came upon a fancy fireman's frame. Since it was empty, and he felt the need to fill it, he painted a cover using the frame and then put a painting into the frame. So actually, the frame generated the picture, and the picture was done for the frame. This frame, which Rockwell bought for $1, had various artifacts of the fire-fighting profession carved into it. Norman quickly conjured up a turn-of-the-century fireman complete with old-time uniform and big, black mustache as the idea for this picture. He then added the notion of someone thoughtlessly leaving a cigar butt on the mantel below the framed picture. The smoke from the cigar came up past the fireman's face, and naturally, the fireman found it nothing less than objectionable. How well Rockwell captured that magnificent visage in this picture within a picture.

THE SATURDAY EVENING
POST

MAY 27, 1944   10¢

norman rockwell

"The War Bond"

Norman Rockwell felt that World War II was his own personal war, and he was going to do everything in his power to win it. He looked upon soldiers and sailors as civilians in uniform, and the war itself as everybody's fight. Through his art, he tried to explain what the war was all about. The result of his effort was the "Four Freedoms."

These "Four Freedoms," first rejected by the Government and then printed in millions of copies as war bond posters, were seen by millions of people. Through Rockwell's artwork, these posters raised $132 million in war bonds in a six-month period. The bonds were as important to the war effort as was saving flattened tin cans, conducting air raid drills, and rolling bandages for use by our wounded G. I.s overseas.

While the country back home is preparing to celebrate the Fourth of July with firecrackers and noisy marching bands, this G.I. reflects upon his all-too-recent tour of duty on the battlefield. He gazes upon the war bond, which he knows will strengthen the future of his country and his family as well. With strong conviction, he realizes that the pain and turmoil which he has suffered in battle will not have been in vain.

THE SATURDAY EVENING
POST
JULY 1, 1944
10¢
UNITED STATES
WAR SAVINGS BOND
Pvt. Roy Cole
Arlington
Vermont
EXCLUSIVE
COMMANDO KELLY
TELLS HIS
LIFE STORY
Norman
Rockwell

"Rest and Relaxation"

Having been in the Navy in his early years, Rockwell certainly recognized the value of a military leave. Not only did it give a serviceman an opportunity to take a break from the rigors of military life, but it also gave him some time to spend a few often-hurried hours with his best girl.

In this picture, we see the serviceman and his best girl cherishing those few solitary moments together. Their thoughts are only with each other, and for just a little while, they will try to blot out of their minds that this leave, like all other good things, must come to an end. The airman has lowered the window shade about as far as it will go and has hung his coat over the window to afford himself just a bit more privacy.

Despite these precautions, though, there is no way to shield themselves from the prying eyes of the young passenger in the front seat. She is closely watching the scene and waiting for that moment when the happy couple will again steal a little kiss. She will then plant that picture firmly in the back of her mind so, first thing tomorrow morning, she can run and tell all of her friends.

Unfortunately for our loving couple, little girls do not provide the only interruption; the conductor is about to pick up the tickets and pierce them with his punch.

THE SATURDAY EVENING

POST

AUGUST 12, 1944   10¢

DEWEY'S APRIL CHOICE
By FORREST DAVIS

A RIOTOUS GOLF STORY
By PAUL GALLICO

Norman Rockwell

"Six Generations of Gillis"

Readers of *The Saturday Evening Post* eagerly looked forward each week to the arrival of the magazine to see if there was another episode of Willie Gillis. In 1944 Norman Rockwell showed that Willie was not the first military man of his family; actually he was the sixth generation in a long line of military Gillises. Great-great-great Grandpa Gillis fought in the Revolutionary War, Great-great Grandpa Gillis fought in the War of 1812, and Great-Grandpa Gillis served in the Yankee army during the Civil War. Grandpa Gillis, also known to the rest of the family as "Fightin' Bill," performed his tour of duty in the Spanish-American War. During the first World War, dear old Dad Gillis defended his country, and now, during World War II, it's Willie's turn to follow through with his patriotic duty. Note that all of the Gillises served with distinction (of course!), as evidenced by the many books written about them: *A History of the United States and the Gillis Family, Gillis and Lincoln,* and finally, the book that is the pride and joy of the male members of the family, *Great Loves of the Gillises.* All vie for space on the crowded shelf.

Once again, Robert Buck posed not only for Willie but for all of the other Gillises shown in the picture. About this time, young Buck almost ended the series by going into the service himself; he enlisted as a naval aviator and flew a number of missions overseas. It was not until 1946 that the next, and final, Willie Gillis cover appeared.

THE SATURDAY EVENING

POST

SEPTEMBER 16, 1944   10¢

Great Great Great Grandpa Gillis

Great Great Grandpa Gillis

Great Grandpa Gillis

Grandpa Gillis

"Fighting Bill" Gillis

Gillis

your son
Willie Gillis

THEY SPARKED THE
CARRIER REVOLUTION
BY JACK ALEXANDER
———
HOW SHALL WE RECONVERT
TO PEACETIME WORK?
MAURY MAVERICK
LOUIS RUTHENBURG

norman
rockwell

"Which One?"

Norman Rockwell first delved into the world of politics in his October 9, 1920, cover, which dealt with the presidential campaign between Harding and Cox. Now, some twenty-four years later, Norman again takes a look at the fickle world of politics.

Showing no partisanship whatsoever, Rockwell depicts the bewildered look on this Cedar Rapids (Iowa) gentleman as he tries to decide just which man he feels would be best for the job. The gentleman is exercising his American duty by taking time off on this rainy November day to cast his vote. Together with millions of other Americans, he will make the decision that will return Franklin Delano Roosevelt to the White House. Thomas Dewey, governor of New York, would make one more run for the presidency in 1948, and only H. V. Kaltenborn and the *Chicago Tribune* would then declare him the winner.

How well all of us can sympathize with this gentleman as he ponders his decision, his pockets filled with political booklets, all of which somehow seem never to be read.

THE SATURDAY EVENING POST

NOVEMBER 4, 1944   10¢

The Cedar Rapids Gazette

WHICH ONE?

POLITICAL QUESTIONS

?

A NEW
Colonel Primrose
Mystery
By LESLIE FORD

SNIPER SHIP
By JOHN BISHOP

norman rockwell

"Holiday Rush"

In 1944 Rockwell got the notion that he would like to do the inside of a railroad station during a wartime Christmas season. He said, "I would like to show the pathos and humor of the mother meeting the son, the wife meeting her husband, one lover meeting another."

After driving about and looking at many different stations, Rockwell finally settled on the Chicago Northwestern railroad station. After discussing his thoughts with the stationmaster and the advertising manager, all three tried to determine just how the station should be decorated for the holidays. Rockwell was finally told, "You create the cover, and that is the way we'll decorate the station."

One day Rockwell photographed over one hundred soldiers, sailors, and marines meeting their family and friends. Everyone seemed eager to be helpful, and for the most part, everyone seemed eager to be in the picture. Beautiful girls were asked to kiss utter strangers, barely minding the whole thing.

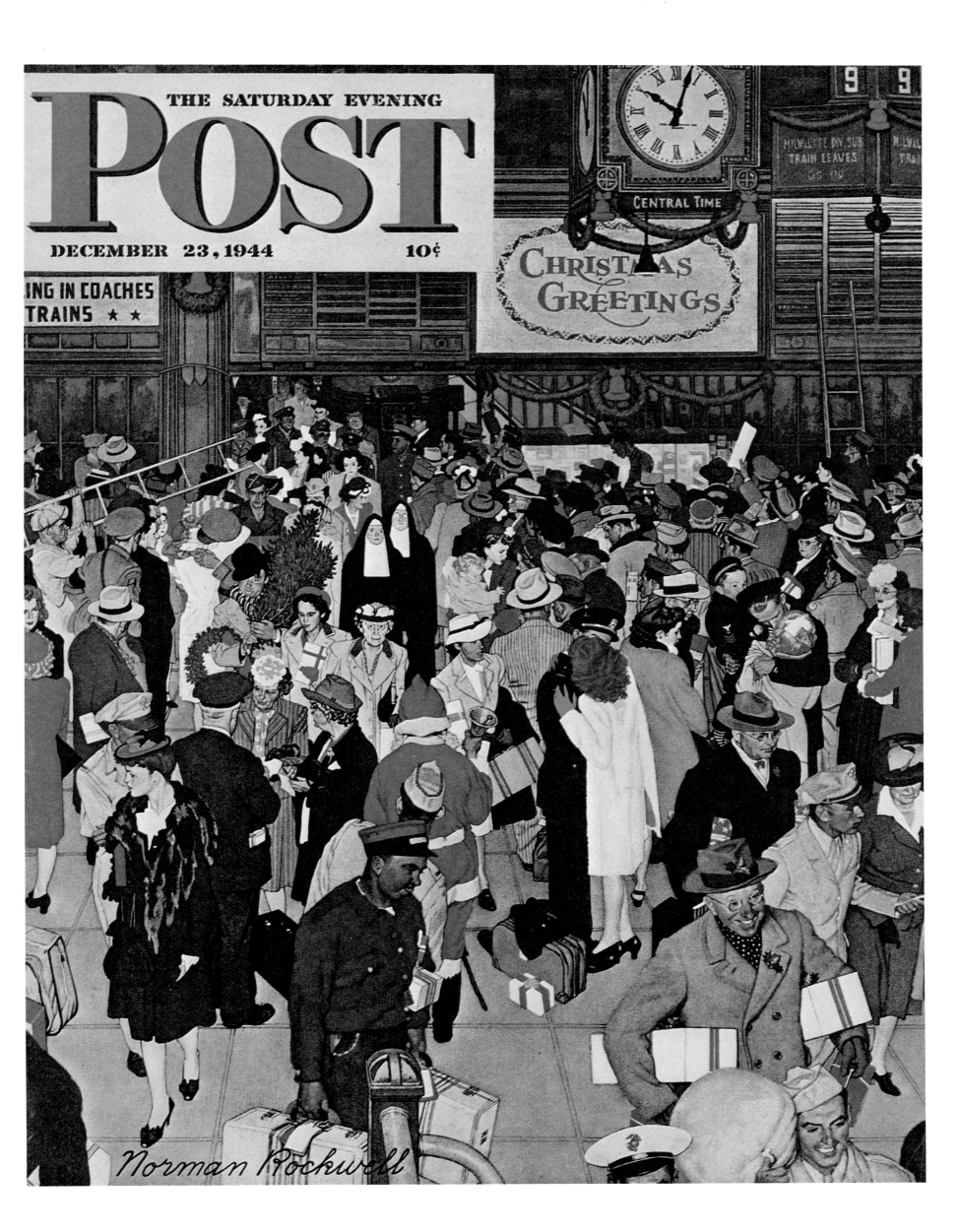

"Beating the Deadline"

All of us have experienced the agony of meeting that springtime deadline for filing our income tax. In recent years, the Government has given us a month's grace by postponing the March 15 deadline to April 15; nonetheless, the pain is still the same. Most probably it is the only time in the year when we wish that we had not made quite so much money.

Norman Rockwell painted this man hard at work for several hours, and it is obvious that the gentleman has a few more hours to go. Note the coffee pot on the floor; it will most assuredly be in use during the night, but at the moment it is doing nothing more than providing a bit of radiant warmth for the hindquarters of the family cat. The clutter of scattered papers is testimony to the fact that the bewildered man is pulling out all stops in search of the one last deduction.

THE SATURDAY EVENING
POST

MARCH 17, 1945   10¢

"April Fool"

Some of the most popular pictures that Norman Rockwell ever produced are the April Fool covers. These prove Rockwell's magnificent obsession with detail. Details, in fact, become the most important points of interest in these particular paintings. This March 31 cover is the second in a series of three April Fool pictures painted.

This picture laid claim to having forty-five mistakes, and as with the previous foolish cover, it brought forth a deluge of mail. Many of the writers claimed to have found many more than the forty-five mistakes Rockwell declared he had put in the picture. Just to note a few of the obvious, one might find poison ivy, thimbleweed, an uncommon tree root, a fisherman in need of a bit more training, an unusual inhabitant of a musical instrument, a strange nesting place for furry friends, and an artist who stood on his head to write his name upside down and backwards. Buy why take all the fun out of it by giving away all the details? Make a checklist, and see how many errors you can find!

Norman Rockwell's List of Errors

1. Apples on maple tree. 2. Different colored apples. 3. Baseball among apples. 4. Pine boughs. 5. Pine cones should point down under bough. 6. Horse chestnut leaves. 7. Grapes. 8. April 1, 1945, cover on Sunday, not Monday. 9. Penguins don't fly. 10. Halo. 11. Nest on phone. 12. Different colored eggs. 13. Phone wire on wrong end of receiver. 14. Different or wrong colored butterflies. 15. Books on tree. 16. Castle on landscape. 17. Lighthouse and ship. 18. Ear muffs. 19. Fur collar on velvet jacket. 20. Two different designs on shirt. 21. Life jacket. 22. Three hands. 23. Shirt buttoned wrong way. 24. Cigarette and pipe used at same time. 25. Collar and necktie on bird. 26. Fly-casting reel on bait-casting rod. 27. Cloth patches on waders. 28. Rod upside down. 29. Alligator on root. 30. Cobra in mandolin. 31. Ribbon on mandolin. 32. Post heading on wrong side of magazine. 33. Snow scene. 34. Horizons different on two scenes. 35. Horns on moose head. 36. Animal head on turtle. 37. You're wrong! There are blue lobsters but they are rare and unusual. Rockwell saw one once in Maine. 38. Tomato picture on plum can. 39. House slippers on skis. 40. Shells. 41. Dutchman's breeches. 42. Ladies' slippers. 43. Buttercup. 44. Thimbleweed. 45. Batchelor buttons. 46. Poison Ivy. 47. Signature upside down and backwards. 48. Skis without backs. 49. Lead sinker on line should be below floater. 50. Floater upside down. 51. Red should be at tip of floater in right position.

The model for this picture was Norman Rockwell's friend and fellow *Post* illustrator, John Atherton, who, Rockwell thought, had the best face for the type of fellow he wanted leaning against the tree on this cover.

THE SATURDAY EVENING

POST

MARCH 31, 1945   10¢

APRIL
MON
1
1945

PLUMS

NORMAN ROCKWELL'S APRIL-FOOL COVER · SEE PAGE 2

"The Homecoming G. I."

This 1945 painting was to become one of Rockwell's most celebrated covers. Rockwell has painted a young redheaded G.I. returning safely from the war. He is coming home to the open arms of his beloved mother, to the welcoming cries of his father and sister, and to the excited squeals and barks of his kid brother and pooch respectively. The neighbors, too, are thrilled by the scene, as they await the return of their own sons from the Service. Patiently waiting her turn and hoping to provide her own welcome is the pretty redheaded girl from next door. She was a freckled-faced, pig-tailed kid when he left but is now an attractive young woman who is sure to provide the romantic interest for the rest of this story.

The idea for this cover came to Norman Rockwell after he read a series of articles by Commando Kelly and Pete Martin which appeared in the 1943 issues of the *Post*. Although the scene might have taken place in the Lower East Side of Manhattan or in the backyards of South Philadelphia, Rockwell searched for two days with fellow *Post* cover artist John Atherton through Troy, New York, to find the right kind of backyard. Rockwell was thrilled with the reception to his works, and he said, "It was of course very gratifying for me when this painting was selected by the U. S. Treasury for the official poster of the Eighth War Bond Drive. More than 300,000 copies were placed on display. I was also honored at the Society of Illustrators' show."

THE SATURDAY EVENING

POST

MAY 26, 1945   10¢

The Story of a
Fighting Destroyer

By Lt. ROBERT C. HAGEN, USNR
As Told to SIDNEY SHALETT

A NEW ROMANCE

By ROBERT CARSON

"The Traveling Salesman"

This August cover was begun on a cold March day. One of the problems faced by a magazine cover artist was that the deadline that needed to be met was usually a number of months prior to the cover's actual appearance. Therefore, in many cases, Rockwell worked on a summer cover during the winter, on a Christmas cover during the summer, and around Christmastime, he started preparing a cover to show the delightful signs of spring. Under those circumstances, it was most challenging for the artist and his models to try to capture the actual happenings which would appear on a future cover.

George Zimmer was the model used for this traveling salesman. If the cover had been painted in July, Rockwell could have easily had Zimmer go into the water, but both men agreed that Vermont in March was just too frigid for outdoor bathing.

In order to get the ripples in the water just right, Rockwell had Zimmer sit on the edge of the bank with a partially filled water balloon dangling from the end of a fishing rod. Zimmer would gently touch the surface of the water with the balloon, thereby creating the ripples that Rockwell needed for the proper effect. It is also interesting to note that in the preliminary oil of this picture (which is on display in the Norman Rockwell Museum in the Curtis Building in Philadelphia), the salesman had left his car door partially open. When Rockwell finished the preliminary, a salesman-friend of his admonished him, saying, "Norman, no salesman would leave his car with the door open." Rockwell promptly repainted the picture and was quite sure to leave the salesman's car door closed.

"Home at Last"

In this postwar cover, Norman Rockwell shows that many soldiers and sailors finally will be doing the kind of sack duty that they enjoy, gladly trading all the palm trees in the Pacific for the shade of one apple tree in their own yard at home.

After posing for this cover, the sailor soon went back to the Navy; Rockwell borrowed him from Williams College. In fact, almost everything in the picture was borrowed: the sailor's blouse was borrowed from a shipmate (he did not have that fruit salad on his own), the dog was borrowed from Rockwell's son Tommy, and the hammock was borrowed from Mrs. Robert Smith, a neighbor down the street. Even the house, which was borrowed and which appears in the background, belonged neither to Rockwell nor the sailor but to another neighbor, Vic Yalo. The shoes, however, were not borrowed; they belonged to Norman himself. Since he was not a cigarette smoker (and neither was the sailor), Rockwell painted the cigarettes strictly from memory.

THE SATURDAY EVENING
POST

SEPTEMBER 15, 1945   10¢

Berliners say:

"YOU CAN'T DO THIS TO US"

By ERNEST O. HAUSER

The Christian Science Monitor

By MARQUIS W. CHILDS

Norman Rockwell

"War Stories"

Norman Rockwell's picture of the marine hero returned home featured as his model Duane Peters. Peters was truly a marine and was most definitely entitled to wear all of those decorations and ribbons.

The scene is set in Bob Benedict's garage in Arlington, Vermont. Yes, that is Bob himself, pipe in mouth, leaning on the vise. One unusual aspect of this picture was that Duane was actually from Dorset, Vermont, rather than from Arlington; it is a well-known and established fact that Norman almost invariably painted his Arlington neighbors. If he couldn't find the right-sized neighbor, he always had available to him a couple of pretty good models closer to home. Thus, one may note, the fellow sitting beside the marine is Norman's youngest son, Peter, and the other boy (under the service flag) is his oldest son, Jerry. Both of the boys appeared in a number of other Rockwell canvases.

This, again, is one of those covers that delighted Americans as they searched for detail. For instance: the Japanese flag being held in the storyteller's hand, the newspaper article on the wall indicating that the garage man is now a marine hero, the gaskets hanging near the window waiting to be placed into a rebuilt engine block, the hook hanging down from the overhead wrench, the tap-and-die set on the shelf to the left, and just above, that which means more to Americans than anything else, the United States flag. The cop is Nip Noyes, Arlington town clerk and editor of the paper.

THE SATURDAY EVENING
POST
OCTOBER 13, 1945   10¢

"The Correct Time"

While visiting Chicago in 1945, Rockwell was intrigued by the picture possibilities of two famous Chicago timepieces: the 7¾-ton cast bronze clocks on the Marshall Field and Co. department store on the Loop. These massive clocks have given Chicagoans the correct time for many years as they hurry through the Loop on their way to keep business appointments or to get to work. The people below glance at them almost regularly.

The clocks themselves are electric and are controlled by a master clock that corrects them automatically every half hour. Each dial is almost 4 feet in diameter, and as they are both 17½ feet above the sidewalk, it is necessary only following a power failure for a man to climb a tall ladder to set the hands. Notice that this particular repairman relies on his trusty old pocketwatch to help him properly reset the time. Note also the patina taken on by the bronze casting around the clock's perimeter. These stately timepieces have proven to be friends not only to the people of Chicago but, judging by the nest in the ornate scrollwork, to the birds as well.

"A Thankful Mother"

Norman Rockwell, having felt that the state of Maine boasts the most homelike kitchens in the world, went to that state to begin this Thanksgiving cover. After making some preliminary sketches there, he came back to his hometown in Vermont to seek out his models, as he always did. As usual, Arlington had precisely what he wanted.

We see here the pride, happiness, and thanks in a mother's eyes as she gazes upon her soldier son. For a change, he is gladly doing K.P. for his mom as they prepare potatoes for the Thanksgiving dinner in his hometown. The models for this picture, both from Vermont, were Mrs. Alex Hagelberg and her son, Dick, a bombardier who flew sixty-five missions over Germany.

THE SATURDAY EVENING
POST
NOVEMBER 24, 1945   10¢

WHAT WILL BRADLEY DO
FOR THE VETERANS?
By MILTON MacKAYE

SAN ANTONIO
By GEORGE SESSIONS PERRY

Thanksgiving
norman rockwell

"Tight Civvies"

The days of advertisements showing airplanes, tanks, bonds ("Do your duty by buying Victory Bonds"), and listening to F.D.R.'s fireside chats ("My fellow Americans, . . .") had come to an end; our boys were finally coming home. They had come home to all that was familiar to them: to Mom (and her apple pies), to Pop and the rest of the family, to the family dog, to their ever-so-familiar rooms, and to the "regular clothes" that our soldiers, sailors, marines, and air force men now thought luxurious and comfortable. They even thought about how fast they would get into those civvies and out of their uniforms. They thought about all these things while lying in trenches in the Argonne Forest fighting the Battle of the Bulge, manning a gun on a destroyer at Midway, or while flying for "thirty seconds" over Tokyo.

When Norman Rockwell began this cover, he found out that Lieutenant Arthur H. Becktoft, Jr., had just come home. Becktoft, a Flying Fortress pilot who made an excellent record in Europe and was shot down in a mission over Germany, had lived to tell the story. Norman caught him in this unforgettable scene when, after being away for four years and wearing the uniform of the United States Air Force, he found that he had matured not only morally and mentally, but certainly in stature as well.

THE SATURDAY EVENING

POST

DECEMBER 15, 1945   10¢

Beginning:

MY THREE YEARS WITH EISENHOWER

THE INTIMATE DIARY
OF THE GENERAL'S AIDE
Capt. HARRY BUTCHER, USNR

"The Morning After"

The ball has already dropped from the top of the Times building in Times Square. The strains of "Auld Lang Syne," played by Guy Lombardo and his Royal Canadians, have all but faded away. The whole bawdy and laughing crowd, wearing funny hats and throwing confetti and streamers, has gone home. The only one left is the tired waiter, who has to clean up the debris in the first dawn of 1946.

When Norman Rockwell got the idea of doing a New Year's scene from the point of view of those who have to clean up after everyone has gone, he traveled to New York to do his sketches in a big dining room of a major hotel. Rockwell selected for his background the Wedgwood Room of the Waldorf-Astoria, and he borrowed as his model the Wedgwood Room's Anton Ashenbrenner. Never before has the plight of the waiter been captured with such pathos and realism. One can almost guess, looking at those downslung shoulders, how Anton is looking at the mess left behind and wondering to himself, "Where do I begin?" It won't be too long before the job is done, and the Wedgewood Room is ready to go for another day, even another year.

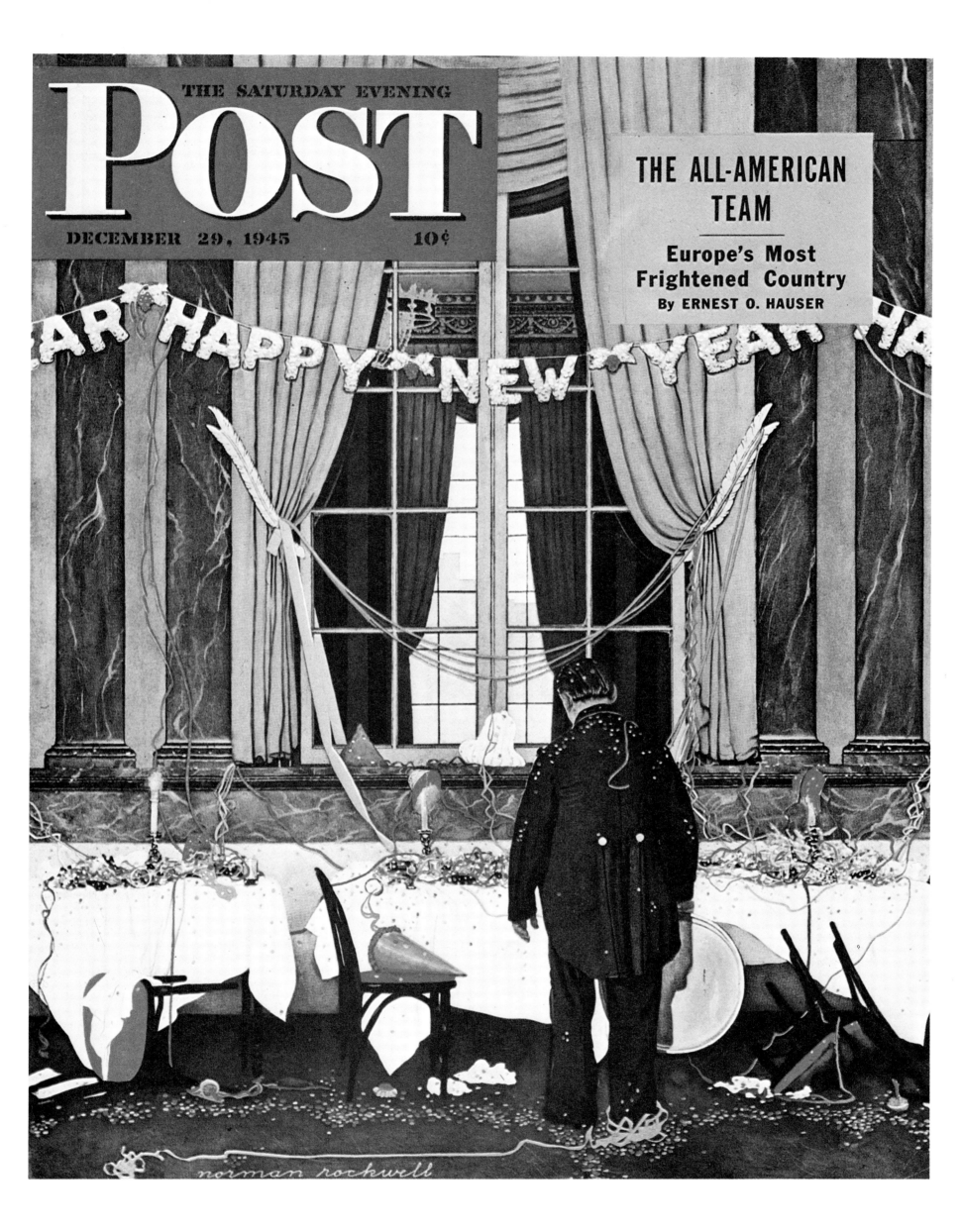

"Picture Perfect"

When Norman Rockwell first thought of the idea of this man carrying a frame in an art gallery, he followed his customary procedure of taking three or four similar ideas and bringing them out very sketchily in pencil in small scale. He then took them to Ken Stuart, art editor of the *Post,* to get not only Stuart's suggestions but also his OK. Rockwell worked with Stuart and previous art editors for so long he almost knew in advance what might or might not be approved. Often he would show Stuart several sketches and ask, "What do you want me to do?" Stuart generally replied, "Which do you want to do?" Thereafter, Rockwell was usually free to go ahead with any ideas that he had.

Four sketches for this particular cover were delivered to Stuart, two of which showed a man with a beard, two showed a man in an art gallery, and one even showed a running dog. In this final version, the very versatile Norman Rockwell tosses in three extra portraits and a piece of sculpture. As was once pointed out, only honesty is what probably kept Rockwell from making a fortune from painting fake works of old masters. Notice that in this picture as in so many others, Rockwell's signature, bold and clear, is written rather than printed in the usual squared-off, line-sketched signature.

Looking closely at the picture, one notes that the lady at the left is looking at the frame-carrying gentleman rather pleasantly. The stern-faced gentleman in the middle picture obviously disapproves, and the haughty general in the picture at the far right is looking down and thinking to himself, "Just another member of the working class."

THE SATURDAY EVENING

POST

MARCH 2, 1946   10¢

A New Western Serial
By LUKE SHORT

COMMANDO KELLY,
BUSINESSMAN
By RICHARD TREGASKIS

norman rockwell

"The Charwomen"

Once again Norman Rockwell demonstrates his love for the "common people" of our world. We see here two women who, early each morning, arrive at the theater ready to clean up after the crowds of the night before. Taking a short break and examining the *Playbill* magazine, surely they must be thinking to themselves how nice it would be if for just one night they could sit down and watch a performance and not have to be in early the next morning to clean up.

Two of Rockwell's neighbors in Arlington posed as the charwomen. They were very respected and respectable ladies, and at first they balked at posing as charwomen. Norman convinced them that they were only acting. So early one morning, they met Norman at the Majestic Theater in New York and played their roles so well that had there been an audience at the theater at that time, they surely would have received a standing ovation. Norman's two friends from Vermont enjoyed their roles so much they decided that for any future appearances in a Rockwell painting, they would let Norman pick the roles and would never again balk. Norman, however, was not always so lucky; once he portrayed a high-society matron as a portly maid, and she never spoke to him again.

Note some of the remarkable detail that Rockwell has put into his painting: the handles of the mop, one showing much more wear than the other (the red paint is all but worn off at the top), the porcelain wash bucket with the old brush sticking out, the patterns on the charwomen's aprons, almost dull but with a bit of that floral print to bring a little brightness into their lives, and the lace handkerchief left on the velvet-covered theater seat from the previous night's performance.

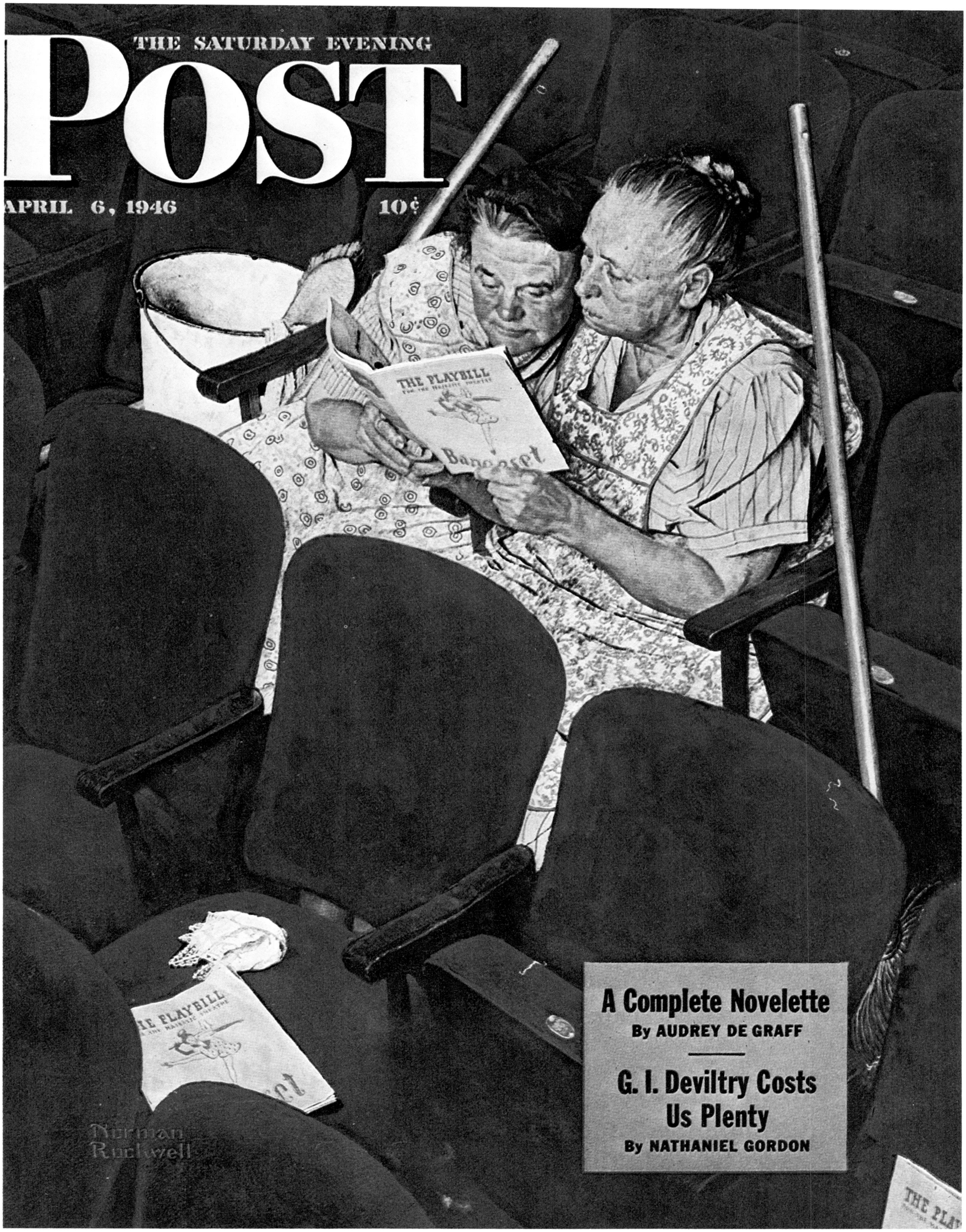
THE SATURDAY EVENING
POST
APRIL 6, 1946
10¢
THE PLAYBILL
A Complete Novelette
By AUDREY DE GRAFF
G. I. Devilry Costs Us Plenty
By NATHANIEL GORDON
Norman Rockwell

"A Facelift for Miss Liberty"

It is a well-known fact that Norman Rockwell had a love affair with his country and with those symbols that made his country the great nation that it is. So many times he drew our American flag, small-town bands, scenes of baseball, mom, and yes, even apple pie. In one of his last works, done for our nation's Bicentennial, he showed himself placing a "Happy Birthday" banner on the Liberty Bell. What could be more representative of America than the Statue of Liberty? "Give me your tired, your poor, your huddled masses yearning to breathe free." We all know what the Statue of Liberty meant to millions of immigrants as they passed beneath her outstretched arm and shining light bidding them welcome to this "land of opportunity." Then as now it was important to keep that symbol clean, bright, and shining.

Every July, steeplejacks mount Liberty's right arm and clean her torch, which is made from heavy amber glass. After that yearly cleaning, the mighty lady of Bedloes Island sheds a brighter light to the general satisfaction of free spirits everywhere.

Norman Rockwell drew the sketches for this cover from the top of the Administration Building. He added the bucket, applying his own artistic license. At the point at which they are shown, the steeplejacks are 300-odd feet from the ground. The torch itself is large enough to hold some twelve people, and the sturdy arm is 42 feet long. When viewing this July 6 cover, Americans once again are reminded that the strength of Miss Liberty's arm demonstrates the strength of our nation.

"Fixing a Flat"

Usually Norman Rockwell focused his work on suburban and small-town situations, but he would never allow this rule any exclusivity. He would often make use of other settings, rural to urban.

To paint this particular cover, he used the local Vermont material that he enjoyed so much. He had great difficulty in finding a shanty as delapidated as the one depicted in this well-remembered cover. In reality, the building he used as a model was a well-kept hunting lodge. He borrowed the goats from a neighboring schoolteacher and borrowed the girls, Patty and Lea Schaeffer, from his good friend and fellow *Post* artist, Mead Schaeffer. The gent who posed as the lazy onlooker was also a friend of Rockwell's who was anything but the way Norman depicted him in this scene. Even the countryside was fake, because as Rockwell himself put it, "You just don't come across scenes like this in Vermont." He added, "You just couldn't make it look like Vermont, because in Vermont, they'd yelp."

THE SATURDAY EVENING
POST
AUGUST 3, 1946   10¢

NO TRESPASS

norman
rockwell

"The G.I. Bill"

This was the final Willie Gillis cover and it showed Willie, now out of the service, attending college. On the sides and at the top of his window seat are his college texts, and his casual clothes show a definite change in the atmosphere Willie had experienced in the last four or five years. As has previously been mentioned, the model for Willie was Robert Otis Buck of West Rupert, Vermont, and his face had been familiar to *Post* readers since 1941. The college that Rockwell painted for this particular cover was actually a composite. The steeple shown was the old chapel of Middlebury College in Middlebury, Vermont. The G. I. Bill of Rights, however, would not allow ex-soldiers to study in that window; it was located in the girls' dormitory of Burr and Burton Seminary in Manchester, Vermont. It is interesting to note that after Rockwell finished this cover, he enlisted the aid of Bob Buck to bring the painting down from Vermont to the officers of the Curtis Building on Independence Square in Philadelphia. Buck was received with celebrity status at the offices of *The Saturday Evening Post*.

THE SATURDAY EVENING

POST

OCTOBER 5, 1946 · 10¢

WILLIE GILLIS

Norman Rockwell

"Commuters"

At the outset of his career, Rockwell felt almost compelled to concentrate on a central figure (or figures) and in many cases allowed the setting to be taken for granted. Over the years, however, he was almost forced to change his view and incorporate the overall subject matter.

Rockwell continually expressed his deepest respect for his good friend Ken Stuart, who was appointed the art editor of the *Post* in 1944. It was Stuart who decided that the covers should present a week-by-week and almost documentary portrait of the changing face of the nation. Rockwell's 1946 *Saturday Evening Post* cover of a suburban train station during rush hour shows us a fine overall view of the kind of setting he favored.

One looks across the roof of the station to an almost Grandma Moses-like hillside dotted by bare trees and modest homes. Overhead power lines and telephone wires dissect the barren hills. Automobiles cluttering the roads that line up toward the station form the forerunner of today's modern traffic jams. The few homes that we see are typical New England wooden-frame structures that depict an architecture of times past.

In the foreground of the picture, the commuters crowd onto the platform or hurry to reach it. Few people are chatting. Most seem to be either reading or at least holding a newspaper. Everyone seems to be lost in their own thoughts of getting to the office on time (or getting through a day's work). Some even seem to look forward to the best part of the day—coming home at night. One should note the newsboy doing a brisk business at the entrance to the station. We can rest assured that as busy as he is selling the morning paper, he will be there busier than ever peddling the evening edition to the weary, homebound travelers.

THE SATURDAY EVENING

POST

NOVEMBER 16, 1946   10¢

CRESTWOOD

"The Proper Gratuity"

Figuring out what to tip a waiter is a problem for everyone. Some people say that 10 percent is adequate, most agree on the 15 percent figure, and the more affluent believe that 20 percent should be the norm. When it comes to a youngster like Rockwell's youngest son, Peter, who posed for the boy, it is a real puzzle even under the kindly eye of a friendly waiter.

In this picture, the role of the dining car waiter was played by a man who was able to handle the part without much difficulty. He was Jefferson Smith and had worked in the dining cars of the New York Central Railroad for twenty-eight years. The dining car used was also the courtesy of the New York Central Railroad. Rockwell first tried painting a diner of the Twentieth Century Limited (which was set off at Albany for his use) but had to ask for another to get the colors he wanted. The dining car that finally filled his requirements is from the Lake Shore Limited. Notice the copy of a Felix the Cat comic book in young Peter's jacket pocket.

THE SATURDAY EVENING

POST

DECEMBER 7, 1946   10¢

ST. LOUIS
By JACK ALEXANDER

A Complete Novelette
By NELIA GARDNER WHITE

"The Piano Tuner"

No artist could ever achieve accuracy of detail without exhaustive research. Not only did Rockwell painstakingly research the props used in his pictures, but he would also make sure that his models posed in as true-to-form fashion as possible. When Rockwell painted this January 1947 cover of the piano tuner, he felt that he would get a lot of letters telling him that the piano tuner wasn't hitting the octave right. Norman thought that piano tuners struck octaves the same as anyone else (with the thumb and little finger), but a piano tuner from Bennington, Vermont, who came up to act as sort of technical advisor on the job, set Rockwell straight. "Piano tuners hit so many octaves in the course of a day," he said, "that they learn to hit a lot of them with the thumb and the third finger so that the little finger won't take the pounding."

Although the tuner from Bennington was a fine technical supervisor, he didn't work out as a model; Rockwell didn't think he looked the part. The artist then had the real piano tuner direct his neighbor (George Zimmer) to act out the part. Zimmer, you may recall, was the traveling salesman in the August 11, 1945, cover.

THE SATURDAY EVENING
POST
JANUARY 11, 1947   10¢

norman rockwell

"First Sign of Spring"

The first consideration in doing a cover is, of course, to find an acceptable motif. After Rockwell hit upon an idea, he would then begin to gather all of the component parts that go into making a finely finished product. These component parts might include: the setting, the model, the clothes worn by the model, and anything else which might add credence to the picture.

It was while working on this particular picture that Norman Rockwell discovered that the common crocus can be one of the most expensive of blossoms if bought at just the wrong time. As previously mentioned, a *Saturday Evening Post* cover that appeared in the spring would normally be painted in the dead of winter, and it was in this type of situation that Rockwell, meticulous workman that he was, thought that he needed a real crocus. Although he called every greenhouse for miles around, it seemed that he had hit on the one thing no florist could supply at that moment. They could have supplied him with anything else that he would have liked—from long-stemmed roses to fresh carnations—but no one had a blooming crocus. Finally, following days of frustration, he located a swanky New York florist who specialized in out-of-season flowers. Without asking the price, Norman placed the order, and the next day the little pot of crocuses came Special Delivery, beautifully wrapped, and elegantly priced at $15.50.

THE SATURDAY EVENING
POST
MARCH 22, 1947
10¢
WHO WILL SUCCEED STALIN?
By VICTOR A. KRAVCHENKO
(Author of I CHOSE FREEDOM)
A Tugboat Annie Story
Crocus
Norman Rockwell

"Carnival"

On many occasions, Norman Rockwell would go to extreme lengths to find the props suitable for his pictures. Wherever and whenever he traveled, he would make notes of certain items so that if on some future date he had use for one of these articles, he knew exactly where to find it. If he happened upon something so unique or so unusual that he felt he might use the item in the future, he would purchase it and put it into storage, whether or not the idea for a picture was already thought of. Whenever a truck rolled into Arlington bearing something as rare as a stuffed whale, a cast-iron deer, or a large moose head, the Arlingtonians wouldn't show the slightest surprise. Instead, they matter-of-factly pointed the way to Rockwell's house.

When Rockwell was assembling materials for this week's merry-go-round cover, he phoned Reid Lefevre, who owned the King Reid Shows. The show at that time was wintering in Manchester, Vermont. Rockwell borrowed the wild-woman banner and two of the merry-go-round horses, beautifully carved in Austria and weighing 365 pounds each. The team was loaded onto a truck and hauled to Rockwell's home in Arlington. Rockwell stated that he not only had a great deal of fun painting these two gallant steeds, but he also enjoyed watching the local boys and girls as they climbed on top of the horses and set out on free, imaginary merry-go-round rides.

THE SATURDAY EVENING

POST

MAY 3, 1947   10¢

GENERAL CLAY:
American Viceroy in Germany
By DEMAREE BESS

PROVIDENCE
RHODE ISLAND

"Second Thoughts"

Norman Rockwell strived not only for realism in his props and in his models but for realism in the thoughts and expressions of his models as well. One day, Norman took a long board, put it out of a second-story window, and said to his youngest son, Peter, "I would like you to crawl out onto that board and look scared." Peter Rockwell, now an outstanding sculptor in his own right and living in Rome, assures anyone who will listen that he did not have to be told to look scared; he crawled out onto the end of that long board and was indeed terrified.

Who among us has not experienced the resolve to try the high dive? The other kids do it. Why can't you? You climb the ladder, a little bit surprised at your own daring. Somehow it doesn't look quite so high when you are standing on the ground looking up. Suddenly, as you reach the board and crawl out onto the end, 20 feet looks like 20,000. The cheers and jeers from the kids below are meaningless as you have second thoughts and start slowly crawling backward, deciding that the safest way down is the way you came up—by the ladder.

THE SATURDAY EVENING

POST

AUGUST 16, 1947   10¢

HIGH DIVE
20 FEET

LICENSE TO KILL

The truth about the shocking official negligence behind the growing death rate on our highways

By DAVID G. WITTELS

Norman Rockwell

"Going and Coming"

Going and Coming" is a prime example of a situation that anyone can identify with. In the upper panel, a family is setting out for a day at Bennington Lake. Everyone is full of vim, vigor, and vitality. Pop, sitting at the wheel of the car, is the leader of the expedition. Mom, sitting next to him, is holding their youngest daughter in her lap. The other daughter is blowing a bubble, which is soon sure to pop, covering a full two-thirds of her face with the sticky substance. There are also the two boys who are leaning out of the open windows, one of them making a less-than-pleasant gesture at the occupants of the car that is about to overtake the family vehicle. Even the family dog is filled with the excitement of the journey. In the back seat sits Grandmom, staring straight ahead, unmoved by the anticipation of the day's outing.

Dropping down to the lower panel, we see the totally exhausted family returning home at the end of the day. Pop is frazzled and can barely keep his eyes open. His wife and young daughter are sound asleep. The two boys and the dog are totally zonked, and even our young bubble-blower lacks the strength to raise a good supply of air. There in the back seat sits Grandmom, expression unchanged, staring stoically ahead. She has been on these excursions far too often, and experience has taught her to pace herself both going and coming.

Norman Rockwell has used these two panels effectively to tell us quite a bit about the folks on this particular expedition. The age of the car and the size of the family tell us that this family has known hard times. No one in this car takes luxuries for granted, and a day trip to Bennington Lake is an important event in their lives. Knowing this, we are moved as well as amused by what we see in this classic two-panel picture.

THE SATURDAY EVENING

POST

AUGUST 30, 1947   10¢

The Great Plains Hit the Jack Pot

By JOHN BIRD

Should Husbands Be Baby-Sitters?

A DEBATE

HILA COLMAN vs. ROBERT M. YODER

"The Babysitter"

The reader can feel nothing but sympathy for this child-afflicted babysitter. The young lady intended to get a full night of homework in on the job. But the best-laid plans of mice, men, and babysitters are soon to go awry. No matter what she does, no matter how hard she tries, no matter what the book on babysitting says, no matter how many times she walks with the baby slung over her shoulder, coddling, cooing, and cuddling, this little fellow refuses to give his lungs a rest. That look of dogged determination on the babysitter's face indicates to us that she is going to continue to search for the solution to quiet down this lovable little monster.

Here, again, we see Norman Rockwell's love for details and his magnificent ability to capture them. The furry look of the little teddy bear, the wind-up clock on the floor, the half-finished baby bottle, the design on the slipcovers, the wallpaper, and all of the other assorted paraphernalia show Rockwell's desire to make the setting as interesting as the overall subject.

THE SATURDAY EVENING

POST

NOVEMBER 8, 1947   10¢

"No More Shopping Days Till Christmas"

Norman Rockwell painted so many Christmas covers for the *Post* and other magazines that his pictures became almost as much of a tradition as the holiday itself. He painted Christmas scenes with Santa Claus, with Grandpa and kids, with winter landscapes, with the spirit of Dickens, with a snow-covered newsman, and an exhausted salesgirl at the close of a very busy Christmas buying season.

Norman Rockwell began work on his painting of this foot-weary salesgirl in the middle of a 1947 Chicago heat wave. The Marshall Field department store (in downtown Chicago) willingly set the stage for him with all sorts of toys, but the more Rockwell worked, the more he felt he needed more dolls in the picture. So, feeling a little silly, he went out and bought dolls; by the end of his shopping spree, he owned $48 worth of dolls. He remarked that he probably had more dollies in his collection than any other 53-year-old kid. Rockwell's biggest problem, though, was finding a suitable salesgirl. For several weeks he visited department stores looking at the help, and finally after finding just the right girl, she turned out to be not a department store employee at all but actually a waitress in a tavern.

THE SATURDAY EVENING

POST

DECEMBER 27, 1947   15¢

A TUGBOAT ANNIE
NOVELETTE

THE DRUG THAT MAKES
CRIMINALS TALK

"The Ski Train"

This Norman Rockwell cover is almost completely autobiographical. Rockwell liked to think of himself as being dressed in prim and proper "city" clothes. Since he lived in "ski country," he would often take a homebound train from New York to Vermont and meet up with a trainload of energetic athletes bound for the Green Mountain State, eager to slide down the mountains. "I sit there surrounded by all these robust people," Rockwell said, "and I feel more and more anemic." Because so many of his friends enjoyed it so, Rockwell finally gave in and took a few skiing lessons during the early '50s. He thought at the time that he could either take it or leave it alone, and that he would willingly sacrifice his share to those who liked it more. The impression that he gave was that he thought it was an unusually dangerous form of skidding.

To be sure of having the proper clothing for this picture, Rockwell went out and purchased two ski sweaters and a couple of flannel shirts. After the painting was completed, he tried wearing the sweaters around the studio but quickly gave them away after he discovered that they made him itch.

THE SATURDAY EVENING
POST
JANUARY 24, 1948   15¢

THE COLOR LINE
IN MEDICINE

Alexander Botts
Goes Underground

Norman
Rockwell

"The Gossips"

Call it gossiping, call it whispering down the lane, call it telling tales out of school, nonetheless, the act is as old as mankind itself. One person tells another, who tells another, who tells another, and so forth. In 1948 Norman had a neighbor who actually started a rather unpleasant rumor about him. When Norman heard the rumor, he decided that the only way he could get back at the storyteller was to put the entire scene on the cover of *The Saturday Evening Post* (circulation in the millions).

In this rather extensive piece of artwork, Norman shows the story being told and retold. It would almost appear that if all of these characters were on single pieces of paper, we could use our thumbs to rapidly flip through all of the papers and create for ourselves an almost movie-like sequence. We don't know what the actual rumor was, but we see that the woman who started the whole thing and passed it on from neighbor to neighbor finally gets her comeuppance in the end.

What fun it is to look at the various characters and try to figure out what their names or occupations might be. For example, one might guess that the fellow in the top row with the pipe is Clyde, a pharmacist. The lady in the second row with the telephone and the glasses is Agnes, a telephone operator. The second and the third person from the left in the middle row was Norman's second wife, Mary Rockwell. The fellow in the fourth row with the blue cap has to be Gus, the garage mechanic, and the man in the bowler could be just about anything a backslapping, happy-go-lucky type could be. But at any rate, he is the one who delivers the unpleasant news to Norman. Norman points to himself down in the bottom row and says, "Who me?" and turns around and bawls out the woman who started the nasty rumor in the first place. After this picture appeared on the cover of the *Post,* the woman who actually started the rumor not only never talked to Rockwell again—she moved!

It is interesting to note that almost thirty years later, another artist used Rockwell's idea to compose a cover for telephone directories for many parts of the United States. This was actually a tribute to Rockwell, as he was included as one of the characters in the sequence.

THE SATURDAY EVENING

POST

MARCH 6, 1948   15¢

Norman Rockwell

"s'looF lirpA 1948"

O ne should not believe the story that Norman Rockwell told to accompany this April Fool's cover. He related that since he had no brush, he made one from the tail of a squirrel, which he ran down and captured in a 10-mile chase. Instead of paint, he said that he actually used shoe polish, which he thinned down with grapefruit juice. Then he supposedly turned his back on the canvas and painted with a rearview mirror. Again, don't believe any of this nonsense!

The cover was Rockwell's April Fool's joke on the nation. He loaded the scene with many, many mistakes, which you may or may not find. Rockwell claimed that there are nearly sixty of them, some of which you will spot at once, others of which you will have to be very sharp to catch. We give you the opportunity, dear reader, to find as many as you can and then look at Norman Rockwell's list of errors shown below.

Norman Rockwell's List of Errors

1. Two kinds of molding on cupboard. 2. North American Pileated Woodpecker head on crane's body. 3. Coffeepot spout upside down. 4. Barbed wire instead of clothesline. 5. Insignia on back of fireman's helmet. 6. Green and red lights reversed on ship's lantern. 7. Beast crouched on upper shelf. 8. Cup not hanging by handle. 9. Electric bulbs growing on plant. 10. Head of little girl on man's bust. 11. Rat's tail on chipmunk. 12. Penholder with pencil eraser. 13. Top of brass vase suspended. 14. Face in clock. 15. Candle where kerosene lamp should be. 16. Sampler dated 1216. 17. Winter seen through left window, summer through right. 18. Antique dealer's head on dolls. 19. Nine branches on traditional seven-branch candelabrum. 20. Girl's hair in pigtail on one side, loose on other. 21. Titles on books vertical instead of horizontal. 22. Girl's sweater buttoned wrong way. 23. Mouthpiece on both ends of phone. 24. Phone not connected. 25. Goat's head, deer's antlers. 26. No shelf under books. 27. Lace cuff on man's shirt. 28. Five fingers and thumb on girl's hand. 29. Gun barrel in wrong place. 30. Saddle on animal. 31. Potted plant on lighted stove. 32. Girl's purse is a book. 33. Only half a strap on girl's purse. 34. Skunk in girl's arms. 35. Sea gull with crane's legs. 36. Stovepipe missing. 37. Mona Lisa has halo. 38. Mona Lisa facing wrong way. 39. Abraham Lincoln with General Grant's military coat. 40. Stove has April Fool on it. 41. Hoofs instead of feet on doll. 42. Little girl sitting on nothing. 43. Rogers group is combination of soldier from Our Hero and girl from "Blushing Bride." 44. Brass kettle has two spouts. 45. Spur on antique dealer's shoe. 46. Mouse and ground mole conferring. 47. Ground mole's tracks in wooden floor. 48. Dog's head on cat's body. 49. Raccoon's tail on cat's body. 50. Ball fringe standing straight up at angle. 51. Stove minus one leg. 52. Two kinds of floor. 53. Signature reversed. 54. Last name spelled wrong. 55. Flowers growing in floor. 56. Girl's socks don't match. 57. Girl's shoes don't match.

THE SATURDAY EVENING

POST

APRIL 3, 1948   15¢

"The Bridge Game"

This was a painting that Rockwell had in mind to do for a three-year period. To prod him along, *Post* art editor Ken Stuart used to clip bridge cartoons from the paper and send them along to Rockwell as reminders. Thus, when Norman finally dealt the cards, his bridge game picture was guaranteed to make a lot of card players a bit nervous.

Rockwell gave North and South a pretty happy hand, and surely Dee Clair, with the red hair and gardenia, isn't going to be silly enough to play a small card from the dummy and let the blonde score with that king. But even if the redhead is slow (Please, lady, you need that trick, so quit trying to read minds and get going with that ace!), she's way up on the artist. If you are aware of how difficult it is to paint four people sitting around a table from a side view, you know how much more difficult it is to capture the foursome from an overhead view and still retain everything in its proper perspective.

"The Dugout"

The year 1948 was less than an exciting one for Chicago baseball fans. Both the Chicago Cubs and the Chicago White Sox finished the season in the cellars of their respective leagues. The Cubs managed to win only 64 games while losing 90. The White Sox had an even more dismal year as they ended with a record of 51 wins and 101 losses.

Norman Rockwell's 1948 cover of a dejected Chicago baseball team sitting at the Boston Braves field did nothing to improve the baseball morale of the folks of the Windy City. Rockwell and *Post* art editor Ken Stuart actually stood in the middle of Braves Field as the spectators filed in and took their seats. Every once in a while they would point to someone, run up into the stands, and invite the man or woman to sit in a box above the dugout. Norman would then contort his face into an expression of wild delight or disgust and invite the spectator to do the same while a photographer took pictures. Norman himself appears in the upper left-hand corner of the picture.

Surely many baseball fans will know the players in Norman's baseball cover. Reading from left to right, they are: the pitcher, Bob Rush; the manager, Charlie Grimm; the young catcher, Al Walker (partly concealed behind the bat boy); and Johnny Schmitz, who was one of the National League's pitching staff for the All-Star game. This game was actually played as part of a Sunday afternoon double-header on May 23, 1948. Of further interest is the girl farthest to the left yelling happily; she was enacted by Helen Fitzsimmons, daughter of Braves' coach Freddie Fitzsimmons. In the upper center of the picture, the girl gripping her hands in happiness was Theresa Prendergast, whose husband, Jim, was one of the Braves' pitchers. As it turned out, it was a bad day for the visiting team as Charlie Grimm's boy Cubs lost both games.

THE SATURDAY EVENING

POST

SEPTEMBER 4, 1948   15¢

IN DEFENSE OF THE RUSSIAN PEOPLE

By Alexander Barmine
FORMER SOVIET GENERAL

Norman Rockwell

"The Great Debate"

Norman Rockwell, many times throughout his career, attempted to present the democratic process. For those elections, he often used old friends or married couples engaged in political controversy. His first encounter with the democratic process came through in the picture "Political Opponents" appearing on the cover of *The Saturday Evening Post* for October 9, 1920. Then on November 4, 1944, Rockwell portrayed the difficulties encountered in the current election as a man entering a polling booth (still not having committed his vote) looks at the candidates' likenesses on the front page of the morning paper. In 1944, of course, Franklin Delano Roosevelt was running against Thomas E. Dewey. Governor Dewey appears once again in this cover, this time running against President Harry S Truman.

When Norman was asked for the real-life political views of the husband and wife squabbling on this election-eve cover (the wife for Truman and the equally vehement husband for Dewey), Rockwell replied, "The husband (unmarried), who was from Manchester, Vermont, couldn't argue much with the wife (unmarried), who was from Newfane, Vermont. The child (unmarried) is from Arlington, Vermont, the dog (engaged) is mine and so is the cat. The canary," Rockwell continued, "is straight off a picture in a bird-seed catalog. The room is in Brattleboro, Vermont. But one thing they all have in common is that they are all good Vermont Republicans. To paint a Democrat, I have had to go out of the state."

THE SATURDAY EVENING POST

OCTOBER 30, 1948   15¢

SHOULD WE REPEAL THE TAFT-HARTLEY LAW?
By J. Mack Swigert

NIAGARA FALLS

"The Homecoming"

For families the world over during Christmases past and Christmases yet to come, scenes such as the one in this cover painting would be replayed over and over again as families are reunited on this happiest of all holidays. In this scene, we see Norman's second wife and the mother of his three boys, Mary Rockwell, welcoming home their oldest son, Jerry. To Mary's right, the young fellow in the plaid shirt is middle son Tommy, and to the far right, the lad with the glasses is young Peter Rockwell. Another famous artist was only too delighted to pose as the grandmother—Grandma Moses. Norman himself, of course, can be seen standing just to the left of Mary, smugly smoking his pipe as he takes in the entire scene. The others are friends and neighbors of the Rockwell family, with little Sharon O'Neill appearing twice. Rockwell liked her looks so much he decided to make her appear as twins posed in two different positions.

THE SATURDAY EVENING

POST

DECEMBER 25, 1948   15¢

HOW OUR SEAMEN BOUNCED THE COMMIES
By Donald Robinson

A New Western by Luke Short

Norman Rockwell

"First Evening Gown"

Portrayed in this 1949 cover is a teen-ager about to make the transition from bobbysoxer to belle of the ball. Soon the flannel shirt, dungarees, socks, and loafers will give way to a gown and evening shoes, and our young lady will be on her way to a magic evening she will never forget. Though Norman Rockwell normally worked in Arlington, Vermont, this was the winter he chose to go to sunny southern California, where he rented a studio in the Los Angeles County Art Institute. Being a stickler for working in natural light, Rockwell was frustrated at the poor light in his rented studio. He had to keep toting his painting into the men's washroom, where the visibility was somewhat better, in order to get a rough idea of how he was coming along.

THE SATURDAY EVENING

POST

MARCH 19, 1949   15¢

"The Three Umpires"

In this 1949 baseball cover, Norman chose to bypass the excitement of the game itself and instead depicted that moment at which the ball game is brought to an early conclusion by foul weather. The Brooklyn manager, pointing to the lowering sky, is delighted by the fact that his opponents, the Pittsburgh Pirates, are ahead by one run, because the score will not become official unless Brooklyn gets another opportunity to bat in the bottom half of the inning. The Pittsburgh players are already out in the field waiting for the Dodger batters to come to the plate. The rain is on the side of the Dodgers. From our ground-level view, we look up at the three umpires standing tall and straight as buildings, and at the same time we see the sky from which the rain is beginning to fall. This painting now hangs in the Baseball Hall of Fame in Cooperstown, New York. The Brooklyn manager is former catcher Clyde Sukeforth. The Pittsburgh manager is Billie Meyer. Dixie Walker is at bottom left and the umpires, left to right, are Larry Goetz, Beans Reardon, and Lou Jorda.

THE SATURDAY EVENING

POST

APRIL 23, 1949   15¢

ELECTRI

20
AT BAT
TEAMS 1 2 3 4 5 6 7
PITTS 0 1 0 0 0 0
BKLYN 0 0 0 0 0
0

BATTING ORDER

35 LF   42 2B

"Roadblock"

Norman Rockwell once again combines the setting and the subject in a brilliant marriage. Not counting the dog, there are no less than twenty figures in this painting. The single act of an unexpected dog holding up an armed rush of civilization actually took place in an alley near Seventh Street and Rampart Boulevard in Los Angeles. The Beacon's Storage Company had a van (which would totally fit the alley), but it was a white one, and Norman wanted a van that was red. The owners had it painted red, which goes to show how convenient it was to be Norman Rockwell. The models, denizens of the Los Angeles County Art Institute, include a violin teacher in the upper right waiting to give the hapless boy in the lower left a dose of music appreciation. The spectacled lad carrying his violin case is none other than Norman Rockwell himself, who took two violin lessons when he was young and was advised to turn to something else.

THE SATURDAY EVENING
POST
JULY 9, 1949   15¢

"Big Date"

Norman Rockwell has treated this composition as a split image. The boy and girl are seen in their own respective rooms. She is pinning up her hair while glancing at a photograph of him beside her mirror. He is combing his hair, ever mindful of her photo on his mirror. Both of their rooms are in a mild state of disarray. In her room, the exterior lighting is somewhat subdued as her drapes have evidently been closed. The boy's room, on the other hand, is brightly illuminated by natural light from the window nearby. After the boy has finished his rapid primping, he will then go to the girl's house, wait for her to finish primping, and then take off with her to the square dance.

In real life, the boy is Fred Beilfus, an authentic bronc buster, and he is combing his hair in a corner of a bunkhouse at the Snedden Ranch in Lockwood Valley, Ventura County, California. One may note in the photo on the wall above the young lady's picture is Fred's favorite horse, which goes by the speedy name of Zip. Interesting to see who is getting top billing. The girl is a real-live person, too—Beverly Walters, a waitress at the Fred Harvey Restaurant in Hollywood. When asked about the young lady in an interview, Norman replied, "She's a real cutie."

THE SATURDAY EVENING

POST

SEPTEMBER 24, 1949   15¢

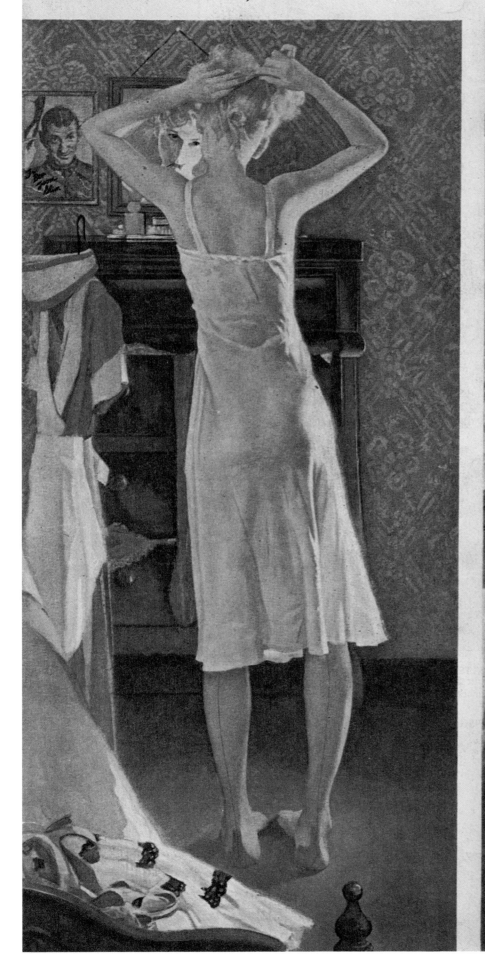

"The First T.V. Set"

As previously noted in a number of his works, Norman Rockwell was a student of architecture. He always tried to ensure that the buildings he drew were architecturally correct. When his two studios were built, Norman was by and large responsible for supplying the plans. In his eightieth year, he met with the two Stoltz brothers, who were preparing to open the Norman Rockwell Museum in the Curtis Building in Philadelphia, and he sat with them at length and pored over the museum blueprints with the eye and skill of a professional. It is no wonder, therefore, that his exacting talents captured the architecture of this house so perfectly.

This particular house was located in the Adams Street neighborhood of Los Angeles. It is hard to believe that this old-timer was once one of the newest and snazziest of homes. It's hard to believe, too, that the occupants of the home would think that someday there would be a contraption on their rooftop enabling people inside to see what was going on fifty miles away. Yet, no matter how primitive the television, no matter how cloudy the ghost of the picture, it will still bring a great deal of joy to those people sitting down and watching for the first time their own T.V. set.

THE SATURDAY EVENING POST

NOVEMBER 5, 1949   15¢

Russia's Triple Crisis
By Ellsworth Raymond

ARE FIVE-PER-CENTERS NECESSARY?
By Kermit Roosevelt

"Shuffleton's Barbershop"

Norman Rockwell had an incredible ability to paint scenes both indoors and outdoors. One of his most outstanding studies of an interior, and considered to be perhaps one of his all-time top works, is that of Shuffleton's Barbershop. In this cover, Norman places the viewer outside, in front of the barbershop. Looking through the front window, we note that the putty is peeling away from the pane and there is a crack in the glass. It is nighttime. The only light illuminating the scene comes from the back room. There old Mr. Shuffleton and his amateur chamber music quartet practice each night before an audience consisting of an enraptured cat. Never before had Norman Rockwell lavished so much attention on an interior. There is no doubt in our minds that we are being given a glimpse of a real barbershop. In this picture, perhaps more than in any other, Rockwell has been able to blend intricate detail with tremendous warmth. Just some of those details are: the comic books in the foreground, the old-fashioned sink and barber chair, the single electric light bulb with the cord traveling a third of the way around the barbershop to the single electric outlet, the banner of the Stars and Stripes on the walls, and the glow of the pot-bellied stove.

THE SATURDAY EVENING

POST

APRIL 29, 1950   15¢

I ESCAPED OVER THE
ROOF OF THE WORLD

A U.S. Consul's Own Story
of His Flight From the Reds

"Solitaire"

In this melancholy 1950 cover, Norman Rockwell shows a traveling salesman in his rented hotel room sitting up in bed playing solitaire on his suitcase. The poor fellow is totally bored. The sample cases, which he has carried with him throughout the day, not only in this strange town but in other towns as well, are piled at the foot of the bed. The room itself has its own air of depression. The wallpaper is peeling, the window curtains have seen better days, and the ceiling is out of line. The salesman, though, knowing that he has to prepare for another day on the road, has meticulously hung the jacket of his pin-striped suit and his gaily colored necktie over the back of the chair. His hat is hanging from a peg on the door, and his pants are pressing themselves as they hang in the partially closed upper drawer of the bureau. The entire scene is lit by nothing more than the single electric light bulb provided by the management of this seedy hotel. As you can see, it is not always true that traveling salesmen spend their nights in the company of wine, women, and song. All they could do in the days of the 1950's was to go back to their room, go to bed, and smack at flies and mosquitoes coming through the holes in the screen. Today it is not much different, except that the salesman will now often go back to his air-conditioned room, turn on the Tonight show, and comfortably settle down for the evening.

THE SATURDAY EVENING

POST

AUGUST 19, 1950   15¢

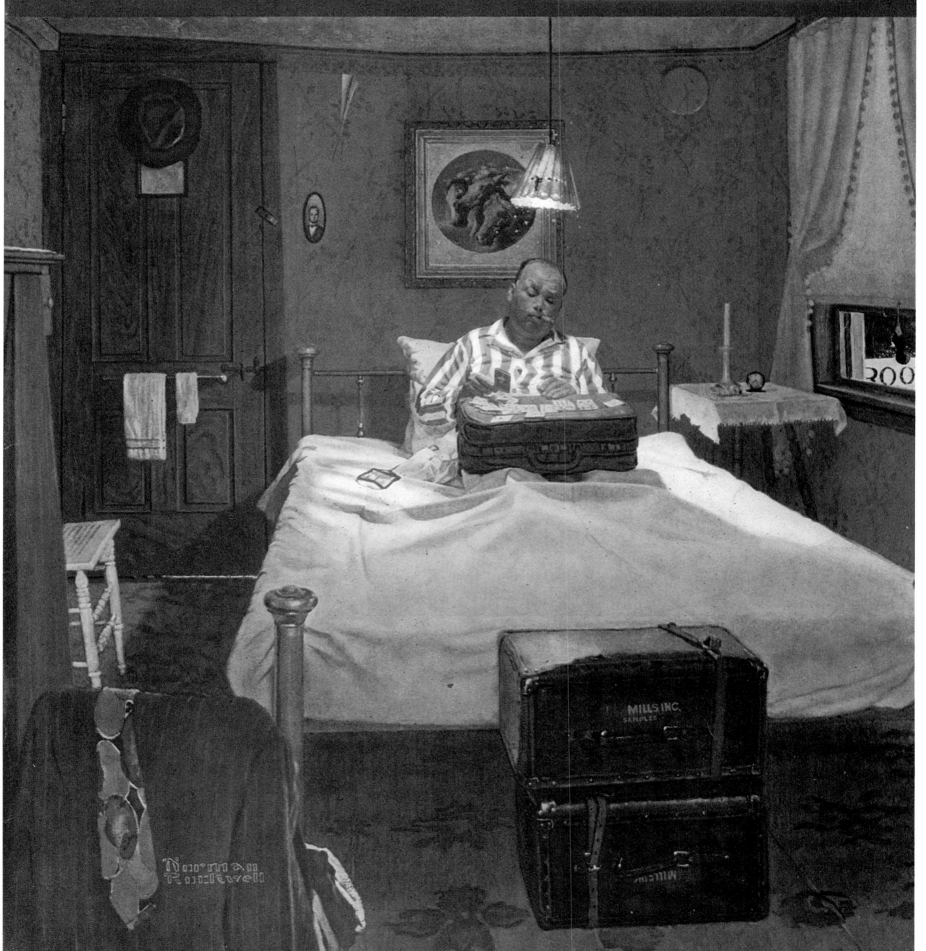

"The Coin Toss"

Whenever Norman Rockwell had an opportunity to take a break from his easel, he would love to wander over to the local high school football field and watch the high school or sandlot teams in action. Being a somewhat frail fellow, he never really had the opportunity to go head to head on the gridiron, but he always marveled at the punishment of one body hitting another.

This 1950 cover shows the coin toss prior to a high school football game. Although the uniforms have changed over the years, this is Rockwell's last football cover showing a 1925 game in action. The objective is still the same—to get the pigskin into the end zone. We see in this picture Bill Jones of Mapleville High as he strives for the honor of a town where everybody has known him since he was knee high to a tackling dummy. If Bill wins the game, he will not be just a local newspaper hero but the idol of the girls in his algebra class and of the mayor of the town, whom he meets walking down the street. If he loses, the gals will go home teary-eyed and so may the mayor. The referee, Joe Fate, blunts heads or tails as the action is about to begin on another sunny October football afternoon.

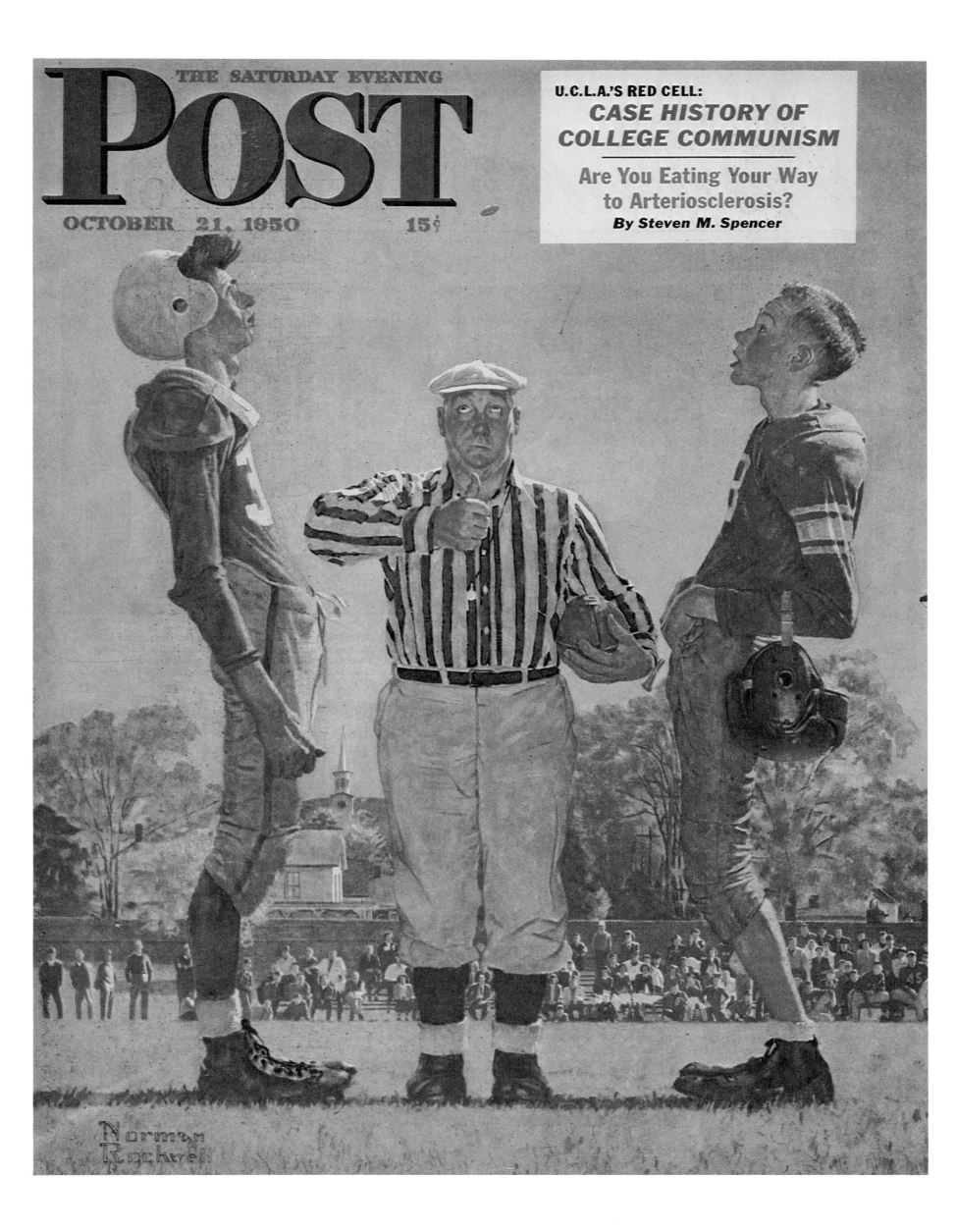

"The Trumpeter"

Norman Rockwell's model for this chubby-cheeked, redheaded trumpeter was Tommy Paquin, who posed with Tommy Rockwell's trumpet. The idea for this cover came when Norman was having a conversation with *Post* editor Ben Hibbs. Hibbs happened to mention the extraordinary body positions his son Steve used to assume while wrestling with the instrument. Rockwell immediately began formulating the plan, and his search for a model took him to North Bennington, Vermont, where he located young Tommy Paquin.

Norman himself fashioned the slipcovers for the overstuffed chair from a painting done by his good friend Grandma Moses. It is a good bet that the look on the dog's face indicates that he feels a couple of good, strong howls coming on.

THE SATURDAY EVENING
POST
NOVEMBER 18, 1950   15¢

"The Plumbers"

As usual in a Rockwell painting, one smiles with the humble person, not at him. Once again, here are the humble, ordinary, everyday working people Rockwell respected enjoying a moment of fantasy in a world of wealth and extravagance that will never be theirs.

When Rockwell painted this cover, he felt that most *Post* readers would find it easier to identify with this pair of plumbers than with the owner of the boudoir in which they found themselves. The owner is gone for the day, but her haughty Pekingese is keeping an eye on things and at the same time seeking some degree of protection behind the wastebasket. It seems almost obvious that the room belongs to a society woman who probably spends as much time primping at her mirror as she does whiling away the hours at the country club. The Laurel-and-Hardy-type antics of our two comic characters provide for them a welcome break from the humdrum tasks that they must perform in crawling under sinks, patching up basement pipes, and unclogging overstuffed receptacles. Rockwell enlisted the aid of a pair of plumber-friends to pose for his picture, and he urged them to bring along their tools so that he might use these as models as well.

The Saturday Evening

POST

June 2, 1951 – 15¢

"The Facts of Life"

It is rather apparent that this young lad, after being told the somewhat appalling facts of life, has heard some of these things for the first time, and he is not really sure whether to be totally embarrassed or to straighten up and say, "Oh Dad, I've heard these things before." Once the father gets through the touchy points of the-birds-and-the-bees aspect of the facts of life, he can then go on to the supplementary facts of how, when people get married, bills come in once a month, how mothers and fathers sometimes feel like throttling each other, how even nice children can be sometimes nerve-wracking monsters, and how life, nevertheless, is a wonderful invention.

It would appear that Norman himself never actually experienced this rather unpleasant task. Peter Rockwell has written that he had a rather close relationship with his father. Each day Norman would ride Peter to school on the handlebars of his bicycle, and young Peter could always go out to the studio and talk to him whenever he wanted—except, of course, when a painting was going badly. Norman would then be a bit touchy. Peter went on, "The worst he ever became was in 1949 when he spent eleven months on that painting of a father explaining the facts of life to his son. Actually, I never had that kind of talk with him, and I don't think that my brothers did either."

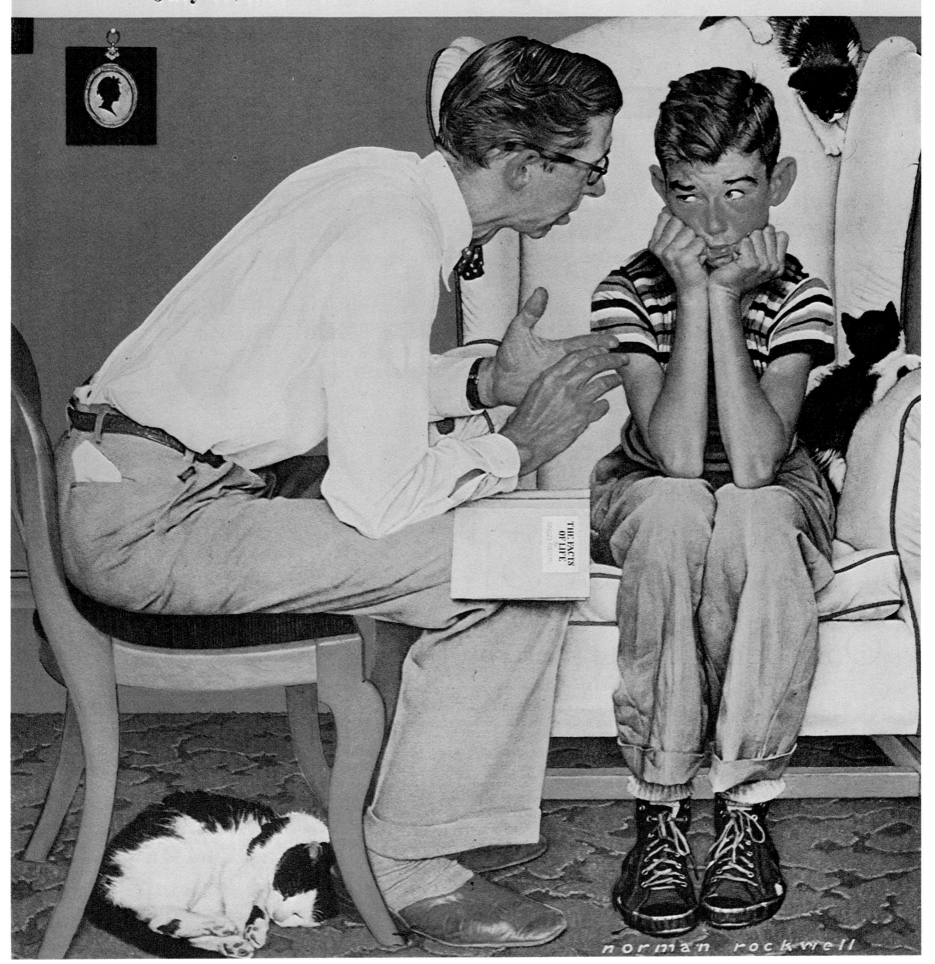

The Saturday Evening

POST

July 14, 1951 - *15¢*

"Saying Grace"

Saying Grace" has proven to be one of the best-known of all of Norman Rockwell's *Saturday Evening Post* covers and has remained so throughout the years. The idea for this cover came from a Philadelphia woman who had written to Rockwell and told him that she had seen an Amish woman with her grandson in a local Horn & Hardart cafeteria saying Grace before breaking bread. Norman was rather intrigued by the idea, and he felt that the scene would make an ideal Thanksgiving cover. He quickly set to work.

His first version of the picture was a black-and-white pencil sketch showing the grandmother and grandson surrounded by onlookers. Beyond the curtain was a flower garden. Norman was not quite satisfied with the setting, and so in the next version, he raised the curtain just a little bit and put people walking by. Still, he felt that he should show something in a seedier part of town, so in the final version, he lowered the curtain and put a railroad station outside the window.

The details for the interior of the scene show the Juniper Street Horn & Hardart cafeteria in Philadelphia complete with the ever-popular H & H condiment tray. In the earlier versions, the grandmother was sitting with her hands together and outstretched. Next to her chair, where now sits her knitting bag, was a brown paper parcel. These were among the many subtle changes that Rockwell made, not only in this picture, but in many of the others he did. Note in the foreground, the coffee in the cup and the soggy cigarette ends lying in the saucer are in direct contrast to the freshly scrubbed appearances of the woman and the boy. The young man at the table (with his back to the window) is Rockwell's oldest son, Jerry. The entire scene is illuminated by a bleak natural light that has been filtered by clouds, rain, and smoke. Although there are nine people in this composition, only the four at the center can be seen as the focal point.

The Saturday Evening

POST

November 24, 1951 — 15¢

IT COST $100,000 A MINUTE—
The Story of the Great Storm of 1950

HOW CLOSE IS WAR WITH RUSSIA?
By Demaree Bess

"Cheerless Cheerleaders"

This *Saturday Evening Post* cover is the first of two covers in which Norman Rockwell dealt with the world of the cheerleader. The second *Post* cover appeared on November 25, 1961, nine years later. This picture shows a despondent trio of girls in a high school gym who have just watched their basketball team take the agony of defeat by the narrowest of margins. The game went right down to the wire, and many hearts were in many mouths among the spectators, bench, and cheerleaders alike. Unfortunately, though, it was the other team who shot the winning basket in the last half-second. The exciting and disappointing climax left two cheerleaders, looking like bookends, totally dejected, and the middle girl in a state of shock. Perhaps they can be cheered up if someone reminds them that their own home team clobbered the other fellows last fall in football. The best thing they can do right now to get over their extreme disappointment is to go off in the corner and have a good cry.

"At the Vet's"

Almost anyone who has ever owned a pet has had the experience of taking their charge to the vet's office. Now this is unlike a visit to the dentist or the doctor for us human folk, for there we sit quietly reading a magazine, listening to soft music, and patiently await our turn.

In the vet's office, however, it is an entirely different way of life. There, everyone sits apprehensively holding their dog or cat at tight rein, waiting for just one dog to start and lead the others in a symphony of barks, yelps, and howls. Looking at this picture, we note that young Jimmy's pup really feels low. He has a cold, not a toothache or the mumps, and he doubtless would rather have two colds than to be seen in public in that pink sweater across the room. Upon close examination of the occupants of the office, we notice that for the most part all the dogs bear a strong resemblance to their owners (or is it the owners that bear a resemblance to their dogs?). Whatever the case may be, this is one of those few Rockwell covers that Norman ever painted in which he put as many pedigreed dogs as we find here. Usually, he concentrated on the good, old-fashioned, all-American mutt.

The Saturday Evening

POST

March 29, 1952 – 15¢

My Personal War With the Russians
By an American Sergeant in the Soviet Zone

GOD SAVED MY BABY
WHEN THE DOCTORS GAVE UP
By Samuel H. Binder

"A Day in the Life of a Boy"

One of the saddest days in the life of young Charles Marsh, Jr., occurred in 1955 when his friend Norman Rockwell moved from Arlington, Vermont, to Stockbridge, Massachusetts. Marsh first posed for Rockwell as a three-month-old baby being weighed by his proud parents. That painting was done for an advertisement, and Marsh continued to pose for Norman until he was twelve years old and that fateful move took place. Chuck Marsh found Norman Rockwell to be a friendly, outgoing, public-spirited member of the community. Rockwell donated the original painting "A Day in the Life of a Boy" to the Community Club for their annual street fair raffle, and it was won for the grand total of 50 cents. As Marsh recalls, Rockwell donated a painting every year to this group.

The story on the cover shows the daily occurrences in the day in the life of a boy as he wakes up in the morning, brushes his teeth, goes through those many activities starting with the unpleasant task of having to go to school, finally dashing out at the sound of the 3 o'clock bell to go to a ball game, noticing a pretty young lady, walking her home, stopping for a soda, sprucing up before dinner, doing homework, and watching a bit of T.V. Note that the first picture and the last are the same.

Interestingly enough, the young lady who posed as our hero's girl friend is Mary Whalen, whom we shall meet in "A Day in the Life of a Girl" and "Girl at the Mirror."

The Saturday Evening POST

May 24, 1952 — 15¢

TRAITOR KLAUS FUCHS:
HE GAVE STALIN THE A-BOMB
By ALAN MOOREHEAD

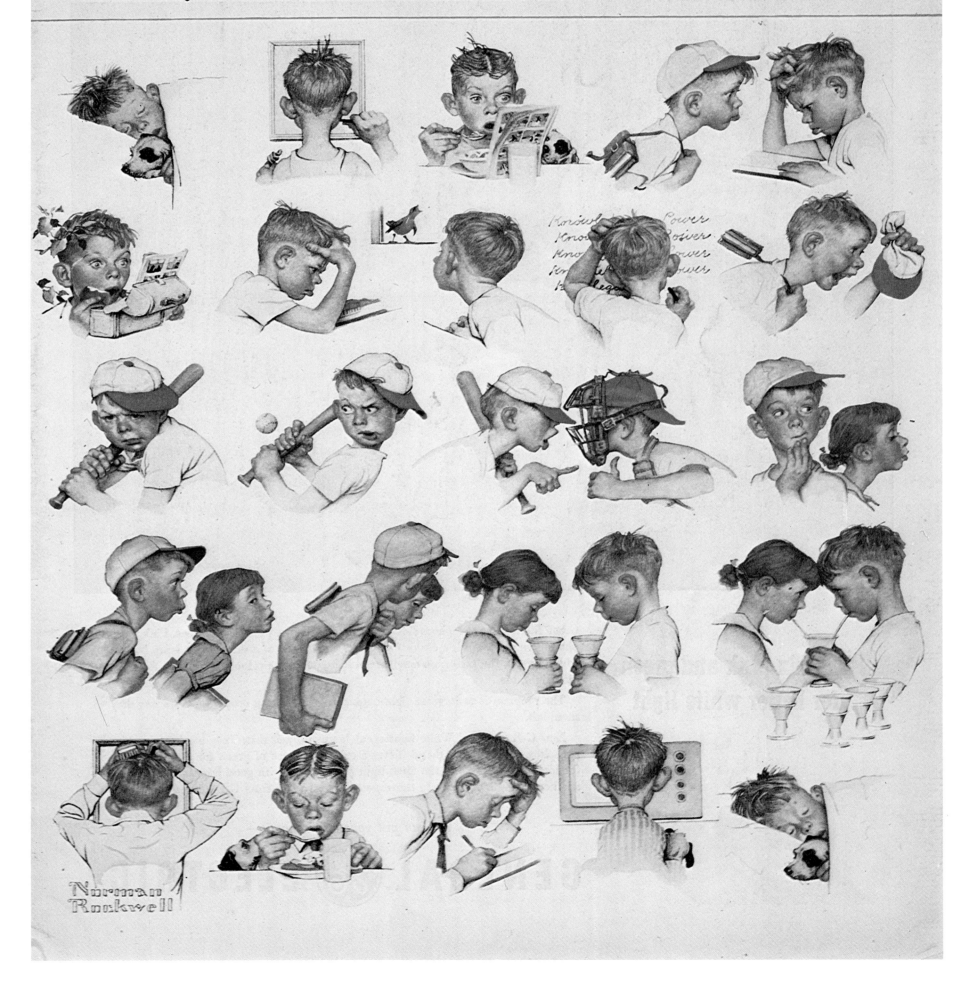

"A Day in the Life of a Girl"

Norman Rockwell called Mary Whalen his favorite model. Mary never knew why he said this, but she did know that Norman Rockwell was one of her favorite persons. Mary has said of Rockwell that he was a genius with a childlike heart, a man who leaves a lasting imprint on people as well as on canvas. Mary first met Norman at a high school basketball game in Arlington about 1950. His son Tommy was on the local team, so along with nearly everyone else in town, Norman was there to cheer the team on. When Mary asked her dad for a Coke, a friendly man sitting behind them gallantly reached over her shoulder and invited her to drink some of his. And that was the beginning of Mary's admiration for Norman Rockwell.

On this cover, Mary finds that there are several ways to a man's heart. The route that she takes is to go swimming merely with the idea of getting wet. By chance, a young man happens along and half-drowns her on purpose, considering this humorous. Mary, who is no sissy, is convinced that she can lick this character, whereupon she half-drowns him. So starts our story of love at first fight. The two young combatants get together rather quickly, and he takes her for a ride on his bike. They share a movie together, arrange to meet at a mutual friend's birthday party, after which he walks her home and plants a kiss on her forehead. Dreamy-eyed Mary then performs one last chore for the evening—writing in her diary about the nicest boy she ever dunked. Saying her prayers, she is off to sleep. Again, note that the last picture and the first are basically the same.

The Saturday Evening
POST
August 30, 1952 – 15¢

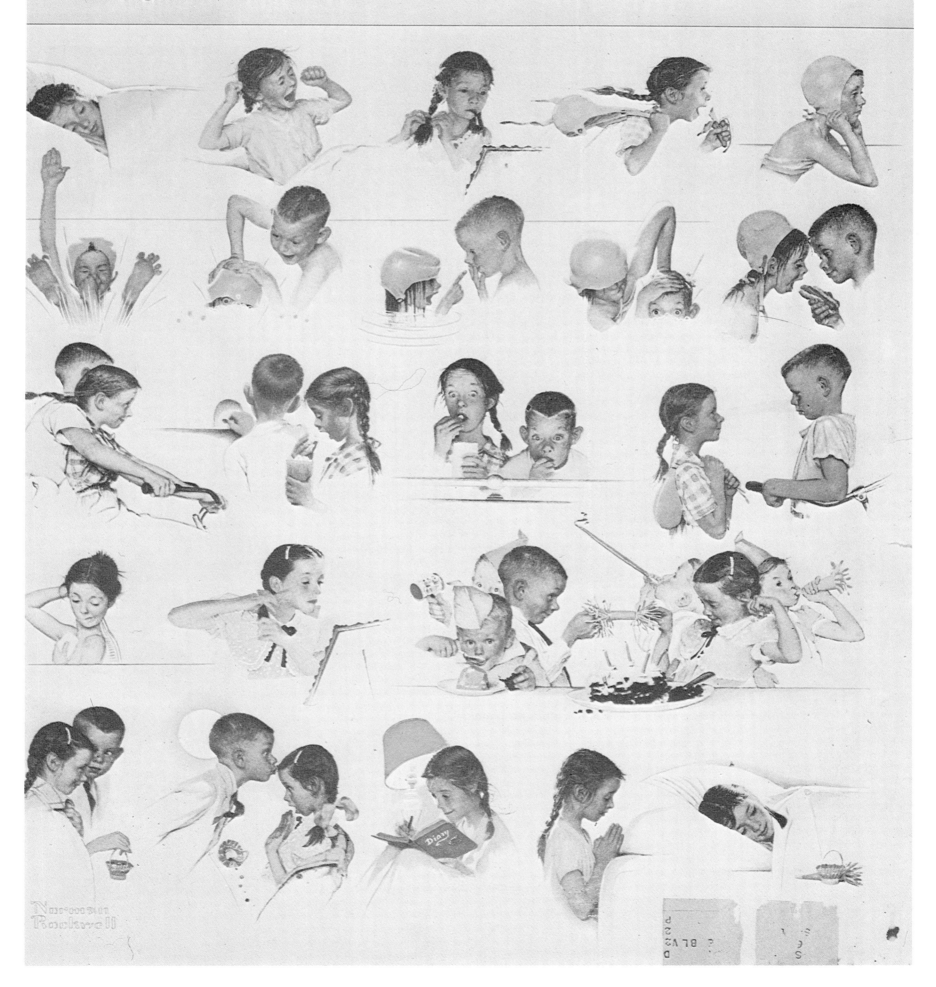

"Dwight David Eisenhower"

Norman Rockwell first met Eisenhower in the summer of 1952 when he flew to Denver to paint his first picture of the President. He later made another portrait of him, which became a *Saturday Evening Post* cover in 1961. Their first meeting was at the Brown Palace in Denver, where the artist caught up with the general in the midst of his campaign tour. Rockwell recalled that Eisenhower had the most expressive face that he ever painted; just like an actor's, it was very mobile. When Ike talked, he used all of his facial muscles, and he had a great wide mouth that Rockwell liked. When he smiled, it was just as if the sun came out. Ike felt equally comfortable with Rockwell. An amateur painter, Eisenhower used his visits with Norman as an opportunity to get a few painting tips from the expert. On one occasion when Rockwell requested of Eisenhower that he flash his famous grin, Ike smiled, then caught himself and requested, "Please don't paint that gold filling in my mouth; Mamie doesn't like it when I show that in a picture."

The Saturday Evening POST

October 11, 1952 — 15¢

Norman Rockwell

"Weighty Matters"

When it comes to calories, a man cannot eat his cake and have it too. While some people do not eat enough, other folks cannot curb their desire to eat everything in sight. Even reading a book on how to diet is not always the answer. Many folks (and perhaps even the chubby fellow pictured here) will actively diet in the presence of others and then, when no one is looking, eat themselves into oblivion.

If those cakes on the cover are torturing the famished fellow, Norman Rockwell should have been ashamed of himself. Actually, Rockwell had them in his studio; they were made of cardboard and a form of icing that is similar to concrete. Such pastries are sometimes displayed in bakery windows to stimulate salivary glands. We regret to report that Rockwell took a diabolical delight in watching friends look dreamy-eyed at his cakes and then be terribly disillusioned. Ah, this Rockwell used to be such a nice fellow! But no matter, let's give credit where credit is due. Surrounded by all those delicious creme-filled cakes laden with mounds of sugary icing, our fat friend is really making a concentrated effort to eat nothing but carrots and lettuce. Of course, though, we must wonder how many pounds of those birthday, anniversary, and all-occasion cakes he has consumed in his lifetime to reach his present state of obesity.

The Saturday Evening POST

January 3, 1953 - 15¢

NEW ZEALAND TO BOSTON
IN A 45-FOOT SAILBOAT:

We Made the Impossible Voyage

By LYDIA DAVIS

"Sunday Morning"

Norman Rockwell was overly critical of this painting, saying that it would have been a better cover had he not caricatured the people. Norman noticed this mistake while painting the first version and started the picture over. But although he toned down the caricature, he did not eliminate it entirely. He stated, "I see the people as real people. I oversimplified, tried to make them too cute. In this instance, a cute little family. I don't, however, do it satirically to poke fun at the people." Norman added the roofs and the church steeple to the background in the final version. By painting birds flying up from the steeple, he thought he could convey the message that the bells were clanging. This, he felt, would clarify the story he was trying to tell. Without it, he thought one might not realize that the family is going to church. One is certain of the family's destination, and, even to a certain extent, of their route—up the block and around the corner.

Rockwell displays here a rather down-and-out neighborhood in one of our older cities. There is garbage on the streets, and one can almost smell the morning bacon being prepared on a hot plate in the dingy room above the Silver Slipper Grill. Dick Tracy, Blondie and Dagwood, and Mutt and Jeff are waiting to be read in the Sunday morning comics on the front steps. Windows are open to admit the early morning spring air, which, even with the garbage and trash strewn about below, is better than the stuffy air of winter. Although Rockwell has shown that the buildings are several generations old, many are already adorned with the newfangled T.V. antennas. What is most interesting about this picture is that Norman Rockwell wanted to make this painting the same small size as the great Dutch artist Vermeer's "A Street in Delft," but his stretcher frame was a half-inch wider. "Couldn't paint it better than Vermeer," said Rockwell, "so I painted it bigger."

The Saturday Evening

POST

April 4, 1953 — 15¢

The Bad-Check Passers—
YOU'D NEVER THINK
THEY WERE CROOKS
By Robert M. Yoder

"Triumph in Defeat"

What Norman Rockwell didn't know (but quickly found out) is that a black eye isn't black at all but rather a blend of colors such as blue, purple, a smattering of green, a touch of yellow, crimson, orange, magenta, etc. Norman also didn't know that the trauma is not merely confined to a simple swelling, but rather is a complicated puffiness. Rockwell found these things out when he tried to paint a black eye from memory, but no matter how hard he worked, he couldn't quite get it right. He then decided to find a kid with a genuine black eye and paint it from life. He tried all of his local contacts, but to no avail. He even tried all of the hospitals in the area, but none of them had a good black eye in stock. Hearing about Rockwell's problem, Sydney Kanter, a Pittsfield, Massachusetts, photographer, ran a local newspaper ad for black eyes in order to photograph and submit them to Rockwell. Before long, this unusual ad was picked up by the wire services, and Rockwell began to hear from people with shiners from all over the United States. At one point, the local newspaper, the *Berkshire Eagle,* agreed to run a story describing Norman's plight, while Norman offered to pay $5 to the bearer of a ripe black eye. In response to that ad, and the follow-up wire service stories, one father of five children wrote that for $5 he'd give all five of his children black eyes, and Rockwell could take his pick. As a topper to that one, the warden of a prison down South wrote that there had been a riot in his jail and that he had 400 black eyes available.

It wasn't long before a Worcester, Massachusetts, lad named Tommy acquired two black eyes, and his father, W. F. Forsberg, drove him right over to Rockwell in Vermont. Norman looked at both fat black eyes, decided that one was a beauty, transferred it to a girl in this color sketch, and the cover was finished.

The Saturday Evening
POST
May 23, 1953 — 15¢

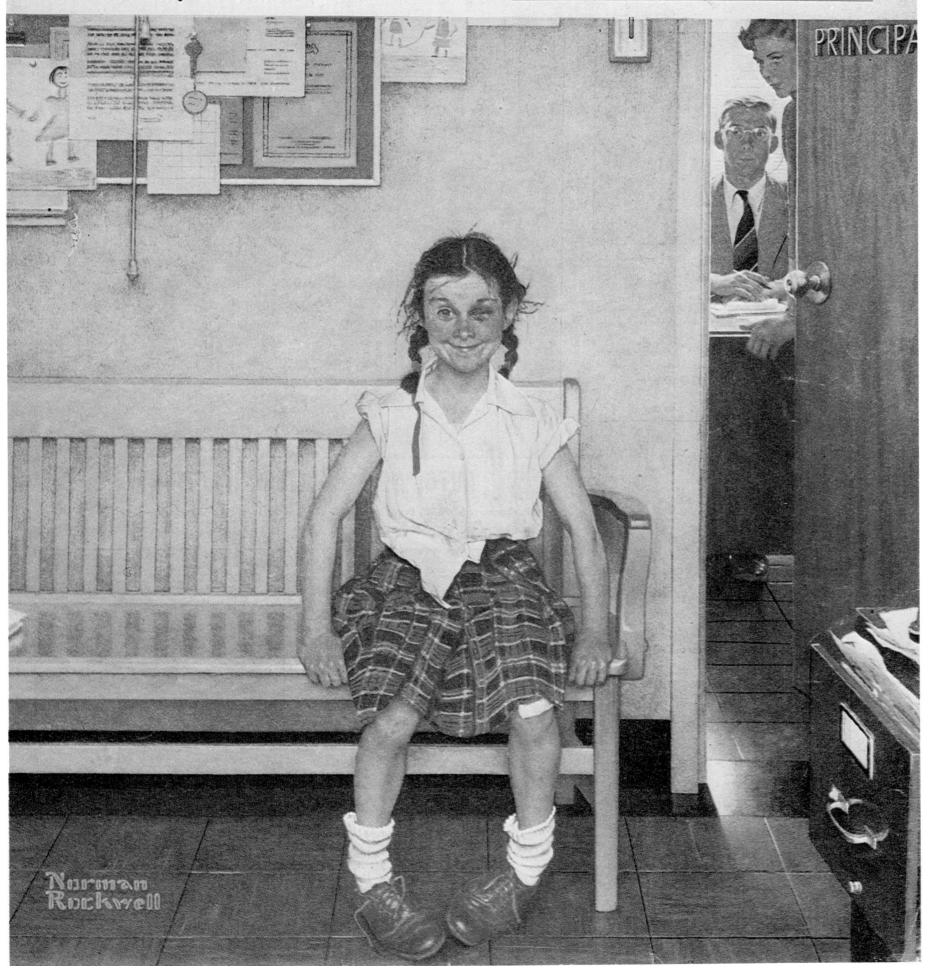

"The Soda Jerk"

As in many of his other works which required repainting, Norman painted this cover twice. In the first version, he had a gentleman in the immediate foreground and a woman and her son at the other end of the counter in the background. In the final version, Norman eliminated these people, believing that they were unnecessary distractions which confused the cover. He finally decided to show a youthful soda jerk, who is popular with the girls because he is in a position to dispense favors—an extra-large scoop of ice cream, a generous ooze of hot fudge, or perhaps even an extra cherry.

The idea for this cover came to Rockwell while listening to his youngest son Peter's experiences while working at a soda fountain the summer of 1952. Peter posed for the central figure but was not particularly pleased with the portrait. "I'm not that goofy-looking," he said.

Here again, one has to notice the meticulous detail that Rockwell puts into his works. The cross-section of the wooden floor behind the counter is placed there so that no one slips. The salt shaker and the sugar container are reflected in the napkin holder. Notice also the look of admiration on the faces of the pretty girls. The chubby Arthur Godfrey-looking fellow around the end of the counter is determined that next year he is going to apply for the job as the soda jerk in order to increase his own popularity.

The Saturday Evening
POST
August 22, 1953 – 15¢

A Farewell Report to the Nation
By GENERAL OMAR N. BRADLEY

An Eyewitness Account
of the German Revolt:
"I LED A RIOT AGAINST THE REDS!"

Norman Rockwell

"The Lion's Share"

At the sight and smell of the keeper's overflowing sandwich with its abundance of extra meat, the proud king of beasts becomes nothing more than a sad and hungry cat. The photographs of this January cover were taken at the Bronx Zoo in New York City, and although Rockwell wanted the lion to eye the keeper's sandwich with great desire, it really didn't work out that way; just before the photo session, the king of beasts had just devoured a large slab of horsemeat. Rockwell tried diligently to roar into the lion's ear to get him to change his expression, but all Rockwell got for his roaring that afternoon was a sore throat.

The Saturday Evening
POST
January 9, 1954 — 15¢

An Ex-Government Worker Overseas Says
I RODE UNCLE SAM'S GRAVY TRAIN
THEY DON'T TELL THE TRUTH ABOUT THE SOUTH!
By Herbert Ravenel Sass

"Bob Hope"

Since Norman Rockwell had always enjoyed working with people, his pictures of America are alive with portraits of real (and sometimes famous) Americans. Many of his family and home-town friends, playing any number of roles, appear over and over again in his works. Whenever possible, Rockwell inserted celebrities in his documentary compositions, including many people from stage, screen, sports, and politics. Norman was able to see more than the lines and the colors in the human face. He looked for the personality animating the features and expressing itself through the eyes.

Bob Hope agreed to pose for Norman the day he returned from an exhausting trip to Europe, and the painter was concerned about his subject's mood. Would the usual sparkling, jovial fellow be down in the dumps from weariness? Would he be dull of eye and dour of expression? Happy-faced like a thunder cloud? To his relief, he found that Hope was always naturally the Hope who delighted the world in his public moments. Thus, the master painter was able to portray "Old Ski Nose" with fun in his eyes and humor crinkling his features. How fortunate Americans are that this same mischie-vous look is still known to generations today.

The Saturday Evening

POST

February 13, 1954 — 15¢

BOB HOPE
Tells His Own Story:
THIS IS ON ME

BOB HOPE

Painted by

Norman Rockwell

"Girl at the Mirror"

When Norman called Mary Whalen the "best model" that he ever had, he said that "she could raise her eyebrows until they almost jumped off her head." As we have already been introduced to Mary (now Mary Whalen Leonard) in other Rockwell pictures, including "A Day in the Life of a Girl," we have been made aware of her modeling talents. As also indicated before, Mary and Norman had a mutual admiration society. Mary tells that Norman would usually set the scene by showing her a rough sketch and telling her a story about it. He would embellish the story with marvelous exaggerations and then in a flash would turn to the work at hand; the time had come to be serious. He knew what he wanted to happen and set about to make it happen. He would jump and shout, pound the floor, or jump up and down. He knew exactly what antic would evoke the emotional response he wanted. When that moment came, when he got just those expressions from his models that he wanted, he would burst out laughing with happy shouts. Mary said, "It is the memory of those triumphant, creative moments which I treasure most. I can still hear deep within me his laugh of celebration."

Here we see Mary portraying a young lady in that transitory time of life between girlhood and young womanhood. She has cast aside her doll and is becoming interested now in lipstick, brush and comb, and makeup. She is looking at a photo of her movie-star idol, Jane Russell. While she is not wondering if she looks like the star, she is simply trying to estimate her own charms. We can be sure that in Norman Rockwell's mind, Mary Whalen was far more charming and glamorous than any movie star, and we know that it will not be too long before that cast-aside doll becomes nothing more than a memory.

The Saturday Evening

POST

March 6, 1954 — 15¢

NORMAN ROCKWELL

"The Choirboy"

Once upon a time, long ago, Norman Rockwell sang soprano in a choir. As time went on and his voice began to croak, he was hastily promoted to altar boy. In this picture, Rockwell's paint-brush smiled reminiscently upon the remarkable Sabbath evolution of normal little boys as they change into charming young gentlemen. As it happened, this little fellow, who will soon be reverently chanting in the altar's candle glow, only recently fell down the choir room's stairs on roller skates, and then, to the horror of the choir master, incited a wrestling match with another soprano. Well, may not his evolution be symbolic of all churchgoers? Out of life's hurly-burly they go through the spirit-stirring change of worship—quiet, deepening moments that neither adults nor choirboys ever forget.

Long before this April 17 cover appeared on *The Saturday Evening Post,* Peter Rockwell was an old hand at posing for his father's pictures. Even though the hours were often long, and the pay wasn't good, the work had its own very special compensations. It was an ideal way of bringing a loving father and an adoring son even closer together.

Again, Norman Rockwell's love for detail in this Easter-related cover shines forth like the scrubbed cheeks of the choirboy. The freshly washed cassock and surplice will barely hide the falling striped socks and scuffed brown shoes. Drawing attention away from such trivial matter will be the decorative holiday lilies and the cheerful mood of the congregation here to celebrate the miracle of Easter.

The Saturday Evening

POST

April 17, 1954 — 15¢

THAT REMINDS ME—
Former Vice-President
Alben W. Barkley
Tells His Own Story

"Progress?"

To promote civilization and thus make a better world in which to live, this Joe Doaks-like character has as his job to dig a cellar for a new house. Poor Joe! By trying to achieve his goal of progress in construction, he does not realize that he is standing in the way of progress of the "great American pastime." After all, what would our civilization be without major league baseball players? A howling wilderness, that's what. "But . . . oh . . . gosh, mister, you can't do this! You mustn't! Wasn't you ever a kid?"

In Norman Rockwell's touching scene, somebody may wind up crying—probably Mister Progress. The painter recruited boy models for this scene by knocking on Stockbridge doors in midwinter asking for members of the Little League team. Discovered this way were redheads Kenneth Ingram (right, with bat) and Scott Ingram (sucking fingers). Both appeared later in other *Post* paintings.

The Saturday Evening

POST

August 21, 1954 — 15¢

One Family's Ordeal:
OUR DAUGHTER HAD POLIO

**The Republicans Muffed
the Ball in Dixie**
By HODDING CARTER

"Breaking Home Ties"

Many of Rockwell's paintings were filled with pathos. In "Breaking Home Ties," both the father and the collie sense that things will never be the same. Norman had a particular feeling for this subject, for its theme touched home. Jerry, his oldest son, had enlisted in the Air Force, and his younger sons, Tom and Peter, had gone away to school.

Norman had difficulty deciding on the proper setting, because none seemed to convey the feeling that the boy was leaving home to go to college. Finally he hit upon the idea of the father and his son sitting on the running board of an old, beat-up truck beside the tracks of a rural train station. The son, dressed in his Sunday best with a clean, white shirt and a far-too-gaudy necktie, waits eagerly for the train which will carry him off. The father, in garb that he usually wears six days of the week, has the face and the hands of a man who has spent most of his life in the fields exposed to the elements. He is lost in his own thoughts, contemplating the passage of time and the changes that will be wrought in the life of his family by his son's departure. The family collie sadly rests his chin on the boy's knee. The boy carefully holds his lunch, wrapped by his mother, who perhaps, because of sadness of the occasion, has not come to see him off. The father is holding two hats, one his own, a rather weather-beaten number perfect for his work in the outdoors, the other his son's, a snappy new Stetson with an embroidered band. Both figures command our respect, and each detail is perfect right down to the bookmarks in the boy's text, indicating that, eager to continue his education, he has already begun his school work for the coming term.

This picture is one of the many in which Rockwell has demonstrated his artistic excellence and leaves the author to state that which has been stated in speeches on the artist all over the country. "If Norman Rockwell had lived during the time of the Old Masters, he surely would have been an Old Master."

The Saturday Evening
POST
September 25, 1954 – 15¢

MY OLD MAN GROUCHO MARX
By Arthur Marx

Terry Brennan of Notre Dame
By Fred Russell

"Rockwell Revisited"

On the March 12, 1955 cover of *The Saturday Evening Post,* Editor Ben Hibbs and Art Editor Ken Stuart decided to honor Norman Rockwell and at the same time give him a reprieve from his rigorous schedule by publishing a montage of several of his previous *Post* covers.

With no intention of choosing his best-known or -remembered work, the magazine pictured a representative array of his covers through the years, selecting a few from each decade.

The 1920's pictured two earlier two-color covers, "Puppy Love" (March 10, 1923) and "The Phrenologist" (March 27, 1926). The thirties displayed "Big Moment" (January 25, 1936) and "The Barbershop Quartet" (September 26, 1936). The fabulous forties shows "The Army Cook" (November 28, 1942), "Rosie the Riveter" (May 29, 1943), "Rest and Relaxation" (August 12, 1944), and the famous "Three Umpires" (April 23, 1929). Finally, "The Comical Plumbers" (June 2, 1951) represented the fifties.

The *Post* was never a newspaper-type magazine: Lincoln's death was noted on Page 2 of the publication in 1865. From the time it was founded as *The Pennsylvania Gazette* by Benjamin Franklin in 1728, through the year 1821, when it became *The Saturday Evening Post,* to the present it has been a picture book and a story book where events were recorded and not reported. It has been a playground for the literary and artistic genius of our country, and on this issue one of its greatest contributers was paid tribute.

The Saturday Evening
POST

March 12, 1955 · 15¢

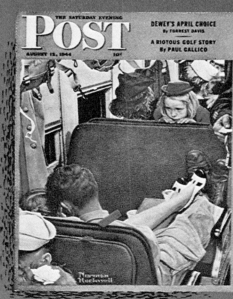

"The Critic"

This museum scene seems to be exhibiting a remarkable new art form. Perhaps we should call it "unstill life." It is altogether possible that when no one is around, those Dutch gents are able to relax from their canvas-stiff poses and enjoy a round of flirtatious chitchat with the buxom woman in the gold baroque frame. We see here an earnest young artist (Jerry Rockwell) using a magnifying glass to study the technique used for the locket on the woman's bosom. Posed by Mary Rockwell, the woman appears to be in one of those time-honored paintings by Rubens.

While Jerry is examining her brooch, the lady (unknown to the young artist) is examining him with some degree of amusement. It is plain to see that he has not noticed the perturbed expressions on the faces of the three bearded observers residing on the adjacent canvases as they, watching with disdain, are wondering just what it is that Jerry is examining with his loupe.

The Saturday Evening POST

April 16, 1955 — 15¢

THE DAY F.D.R. DIED
By a Former White House Secretary

Germany Faces the Facts
By CHANCELLOR ADENAUER

norman rockwell

"The Marriage License"

In this painting, one of Norman Rockwell's finest works, Norman shows the contrast between the young couple applying for a marriage license and the elderly clerk who has seen it all a thousand times before. One would almost believe that one day long ago when the building was just completed, the clerk began working. One notes the book shelves filled with dusty volumes, which have probably been unopened for years, on one side of the picture and the ornate, pot-bellied stove on the other. Paint is peeling from the dingy walls, and evidently the clerk is a poor shot, for every cigarette that was thrown at the urn has missed and is lying on the floor. The license clerk is gazing dreamily at nothing, half-bored, half-dazed; romance is routine to him.

Jason Braman, a Stockbridge citizen, was the model for the clerk. The young couple were actually engaged at the time of the posing and were married soon after. Although the sun is brightly shining outside the window, the clerk came to work prepared for inclement weather, as he has rubbers on his feet and his umbrella is hanging by his hat and coat. Francis Mahoney and Joan Lahart of nearby Lee, Massachusetts, did not wait for the *Post* to come out with their pictures on the cover, since their wedding invitations were dated May 21. It is perfectly understandable that the marriage-license clerk is showing just a bit of impatience, as it is Saturday afternoon (note the calendar date) and almost 4 o'clock (shown by the partially hidden clock in the wall). His day has ended, and he wants to go home. The young couple, however, are not about to rush this momentous occasion. Norman Rockwell once pointed to Francis Mahoney in this picture and said, "You know, this is a self-portrait of myself. At least that is what I would have liked to look like if I had had the opportunity."

The Saturday Evening

POST

June 11, 1955 – 15¢

"Unexpected Catch"

This was to have been perhaps Norman's most controversial *Saturday Evening Post* cover; well, at least it caused a mild storm of controversy. Many letters both pro and con were received by the *Post* and printed in the "Letters to the Editor" department in follow-up issues. Among many of the statements and outcries, were the following: "[Because of your cover] you have reduced your magazine to one to which any decent American would rather be without or hide because of the obscene picture on the cover," S. L., Worcester, Massachusetts; "Do not like lobsters, but think mermaid O.K.," J. L. C., Margate City, New Jersey; "Norman Rockwell couldn't draw an obscene picture!!!" Mrs. J. E. G., Fairhope, Alabama; "What bait is best? Do I need a license? Do they keep well or spoil readily?" A. M., Three Rivers, Michigan; "What did you expect a mermaid to wear? A sweatshirt?" Mrs. M. H. W., Tangent, Oregon; "Now that this cover has appeared, I am not only wondering about the artist (whom I've always considered wonderful), but I am also wondering about the editors who would let such a cover be published," P. N., Schenectady, New York.

After all of these letters were compiled, the vote taken at press time was as follows: in poor taste, 11; obscene, 21; not obscene, 245. If this cover by Norman Rockwell were considered obscene in any way, then the great masters Rubens and Goya should have been ashamed of themselves. As one gazes at the lobsterman, it would almost appear as if he were in a state of shock over his rather unusual and unexpected catch. The lady in question seems bemused by the entire situation. Of course, the lobsterman has not yet solved the problem of what to do with her or where to keep her when he gets home. And how does he go about explaining her to his wife and family?

The Saturday Evening

POST

August 20, 1955 – 15¢

I THOUGHT I'D NEVER GET HOME
Jet Pilot Ed Heller's Own Story of His
Ordeal in a Chinese Prison

**THE GREAT DAZZY VANCE TELLS
WHAT AILS TODAY'S PITCHERS**

"Happy Birthday, Miss Jones"

Norman Rockwell had a favorite schoolteacher in his youth: Miss Julia Smith. She had taught him many subjects and had encouraged him to draw. This cover was a tribute to all schoolteachers and to Miss Smith in particular.

First Rockwell posed the children in a local school. The birthday presents—the apple, an orange, flowers, and packages tied with string—were next set on top of the desk. Then Norman posed his model, Anne Braman, against the blackboard. His late wife, Mary, was present at the time and did not care for the shoes that Anne Braman was wearing. She suggested that Anne put on hers, which were at least two sizes too large. What is rather interesting is that while the children were setting up this surprise party, they decided to while away the time by having an eraser fight (as evidenced by the eraser and the splash of chalk dust on the floor). The young man in the foreground was not able to move quickly enough when Miss Jones walked in, and so he is left with an eraser perched atop his head and the hope that Miss Jones will be so overwhelmed by her surprise that she will not notice his unusual wearing apparel. By tomorrow, the quiet postures of the young scholars will have deteriorated into normal squirms, and the teacher's smile will also have deteriorated. But right now, Norman Rockwell has captured that moment when Miss Jones knows that she loves those kids, and the kids know that they love "Jonesey."

The Saturday Evening
POST
March 17, 1956 – 15¢

"The Optometrist"

When Norman Rockwell was a youth, he was taken against his wishes to an eye doctor because his vision wasn't up to par. He was most distressed about having to become a "four-eyes." When the good doctor, instead of rigging him up with the egg-shaped lenses common in those days, gave him round, moonlike specs (which were just then becoming chic), Norman's pals made him even madder by naming him "Moonie." Being able to see, "Moonie" became a painter, and the pain of that nickname floated out of his subconscious and became a painting. So hoorah for glasses. As for you, Red, on the cover, aren't you happy that glasses will now help you to improve your school marks? You say, "Naw." Well, how about improving your batting average? Is it imagination or did Red's face relax a little then?

Norman had another nickname that used to bother him, and that name derived from his middle name: Perceval. This name came about when Norman's mother decided to name her infant son after an English ancestor of whom she was very proud—Sir Norman Perceval. His claim to fame was that he reputedly kicked Guy Fawkes down the stairs in the Tower of London after Fawkes tried to blow up the House of Lords. Norman always had an intense dislike for the name Perceval and generally used to sign his name "Norman P. Rockwell," especially in his early years. One time as a boy, a rather unkind chum found out what his middle name was and began to call him "Mercy Percy." Norman resolved then and there to drop the Perceval altogether. In some of his early works, however, his name does appear as "Norman P. Rockwell."

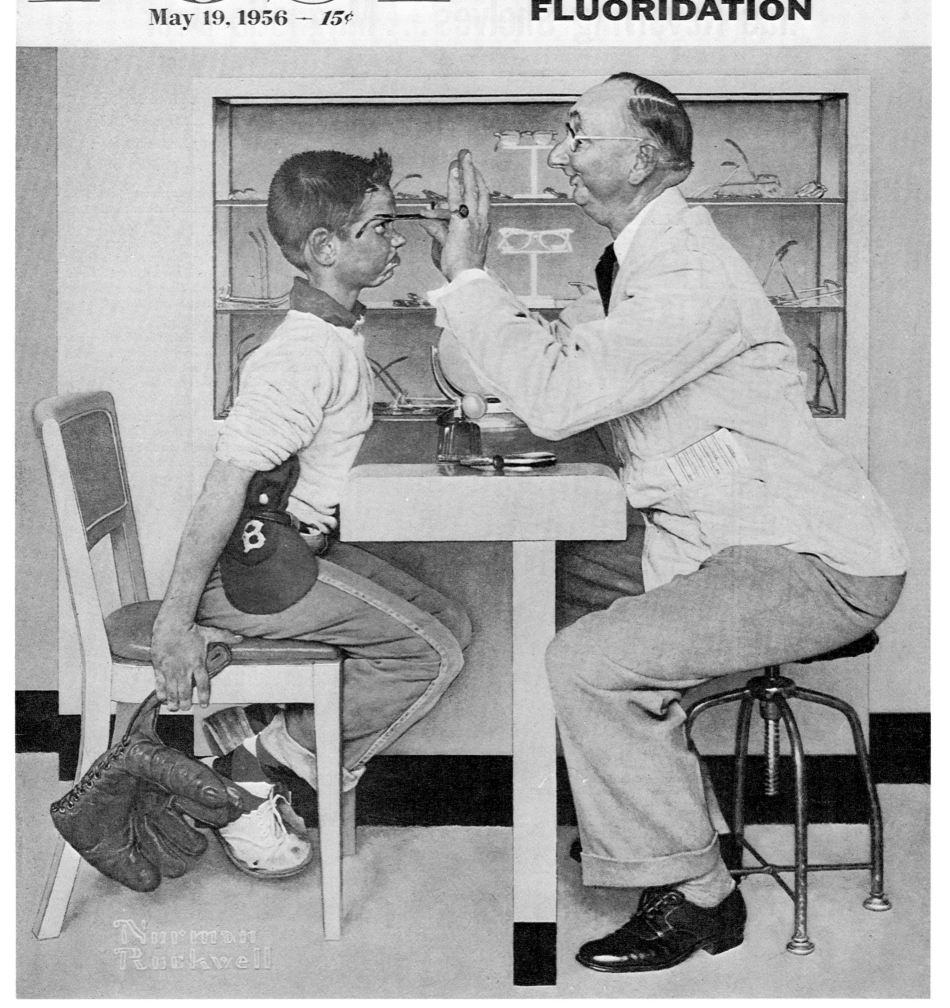

The Saturday Evening

POST

May 19, 1956 – 15¢

"Adlai Stevenson"

Although Norman Rockwell often appeared to have magic in his brush, he couldn't just wave it like a wand and have a painting spring up onto his canvas. A portrait like the one on this cover took a bit of time. In midsummer, Rockwell managed to pin down for a color sketching the busy front-runner for the Democratic presidential nomination, Adlai Stevenson. He met with the candidate while Stevenson was snatching a breather on his Illinois farm. Norman went with his wife, Mary, to Stevenson's farm. They had a wonderful time sitting with the Stevenson family, chatting about this and that, and sipping root beer. "Mr. Stevenson is so likable," said the painter, and then added the adjectives "amiable, kind, unpretentious, and quietly charming." Rockwell, when sketching, must have charmed the candidate as well. He did not pose or "mug," but just sat back and reflected the true Adlai Stevenson. Norman, however, found him on the hard side to draw; Stevenson was generally round-featured, and it was difficult to get hold of the anatomical details of a face whose lines were mostly turning regularly. The opposite is a "craggy" face like that of Abraham Lincoln, which is easy to draw. When Norman mentioned this difference to Stevenson and said, "I never had much trouble drawing that other Illinois fellow," Stevenson rolled back his head and roared with laughter.

The Saturday Evening
POST
October 6, 1956 · 15¢

The Case for The Democrats
By Speaker SAM RAYBURN

Next Week: The Case for the Republicans
By Minority Leader Joe Martin

Norman Rockwell

"Ike"

As was pointed out on the earlier cover of Ike, Rockwell and Eisenhower got along famously, as Eisenhower used the occasions of their meetings as opportunities to get some painting tips from the expert. On their following visit, Rockwell recalled, "The second time I painted him, he took me up to his study in Gettysburg and showed me some of his pictures. They were terrible. His stuff was not quite as good as Churchill's, who was also an amateur artist, you know, but he was a wonderful man. I guess I liked painting him best of all the presidents. Yea, Ike was as comfortable as an old shoe. Maybe that's why the two of us got along so well." You will note in this picture that Rockwell was very careful to paint Ike with his million-dollar smile but without showing that gold tooth.

The Saturday Evening

POST

October 13, 1956 ~ *15¢*

The Case for The Republicans

By Minority Leader JOE MARTIN

Norman Rockwell

"The Discovery"

Norman Rockwell definitely holds the crown as the all-time master of Christmas illustrations. No one has produced more variations on the theme than he has. He has painted everything from traditional Santa subjects to the rush of a Chicago train station to the peace and quiet of a newsstand during the holiday.

In this year's Christmas cover, Rockwell shows young Scott Ingram having just discovered Santa's outfit in the lower drawer of Pop's bureau. That look of surprise and disillusionment is magnificent indeed. Scott, discussing his role, said that being a subject of a Rockwell cover had changed his life. He never considered himself a celebrity, but he received quite a bit of fan mail, made a television appearance with Rockwell on the Hallmark Hall of Fame, autographed pictures and books, and has always been a source of conversation. Scott added that he not only enjoyed working as a model, but he always looked forward to his treat of a milkshake at the end of each session. What is most interesting about this picture is not only the beautiful look of surprise on Scott's face, but the way Norman was able to capture on canvas the burl-like wood effect of the bureau behind the boy. Note also that Norman could have made life simple for himself by closing the bedroom door. Instead, he chose to leave that door open so that one might look out into the hallway and into the room across the way. In the original painting, through the window of the house next door, we see the wallpaper in total detail.

The Saturday Evening
POST
December 29, 1956 ~ 15¢

INSIDE DANNEMORA PRISON
By HAL BURTON
A Short Story by Cameron Hawley

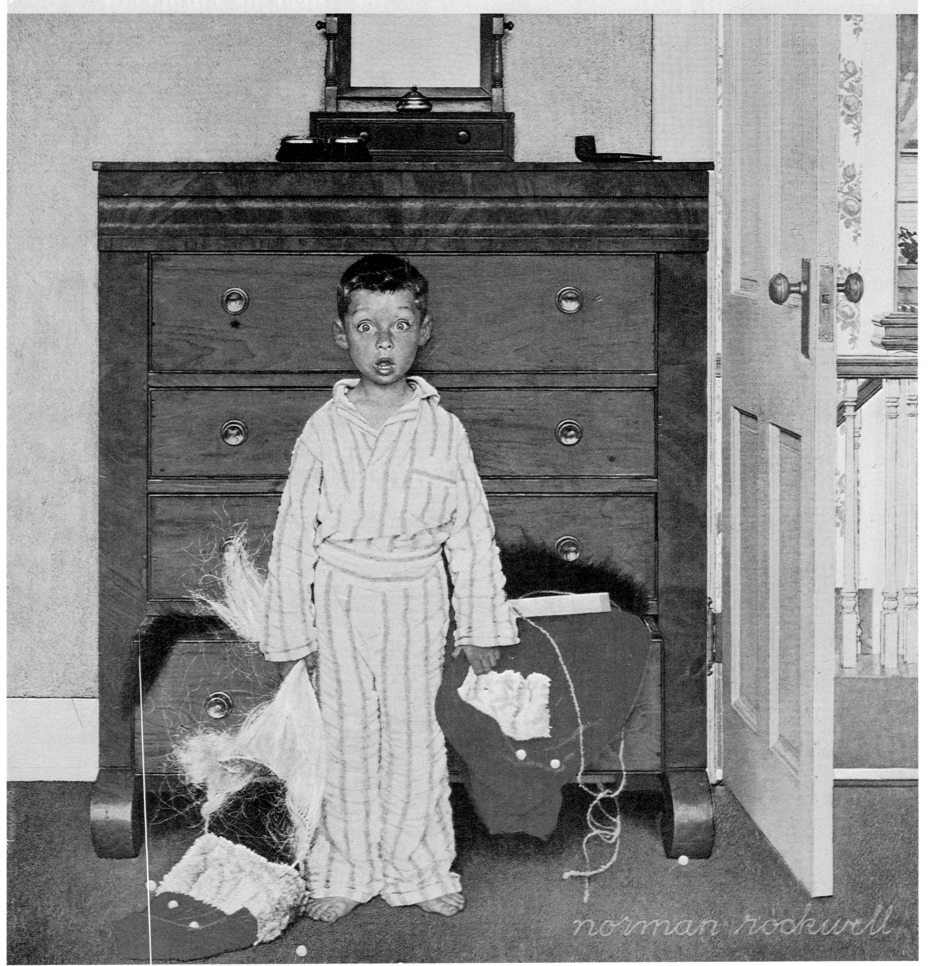

"The Rookie"

Since Norman Rockwell had been a New Englander most of his adult life and had lived in Massachusetts since 1953, there was never any question that any baseball team that he would put on the cover of *The Saturday Evening Post* would have to be the Boston Red Sox. As noted by the palm trees outside the window of the locker room, this picture was done during spring training, and all eyes are on the rookie prospect who has just arrived at camp—all eyes but those of the great Ted Williams, who perhaps has been through this scene too many times before to allow for much of a display of curiosity.

Rockwell used the baseball theme many times before, as he knew that Americans related to baseball almost as much as they related to Rockwell. The players shown are: Sammy White at lower left, Frank Sullivan and Jackie Jensen on the bench, and Billy Goodman wiping away the smile. All of these gentlemen visited Rockwell one day, posed, and met his neighbors, putting Norman in solid with all the folks in town. Since Ted Williams couldn't come to pose, a stand-in played his position in top center, and Rockwell used his collection of bubble gum cards to get Williams' face just right. The rookie was local baseball star Sherman Safford. Finally, at top left (as Norman called him) is John J. Anonymous, who once tried out for the Red Sox and waited years to be called, and who was overjoyed when manager Rockwell put him on the team.

The Saturday Evening

POST

March 2, 1957 – 15¢

THE SIXTH FLEET
Watchdog of the World's Most Troubled Area

"After the Prom"

In "After the Prom," Norman Rockwell gives us the happy ending to the story, but we must reconstruct for ourselves the events which led up to it. We can imagine how the evening began as the white-jacketed fellow waited at the bottom of the stairs as his starry-eyed date walked down feeling something like a princess. We can picture the prom itself with young couples dancing merrily as they tried to keep up with the splashes of light radiating from the multi-mirrored ball hanging at the center of the room. The topper of the evening, of course, is going out to dine at the end of the dance. But alas! The rental of the tux and the young lady's corsage have put such a dent in the young man's budget that the only place he can afford to take her is the local truck stop. The counterman, realizing the importance of the occasion, graciously admires the lady's corsage. She and her gentleman, so sophisticated and so much in love, will have the charm of this night linger in a nook of memory whether some day they will marry each other or two other equally nice people. By the way, Mr. Anonymous (who posed on the left side of Rockwell's March 2 baseball cover) is on the stool.

The Saturday Evening

POST

May 25, 1957 – 15¢

I Call on Groucho
By PETE MARTIN

How Will America Behave
IF H-BOMBS FALL?

"Just Married"

A brand-new Mr. and Mrs. have just checked out of the hotel room, leaving an afterglow of warmth which brides and grooms stir in every heart. They have left behind also the curious debris that seems to follow behind "just marrieds." Some day, perhaps, humans will think of a more tenderly romantic symbol than a decrepit old shoe. At least, however, these honeymooners seem to have escaped being assaulted with rice by their loved ones. Confetti is a far better farewell missile, and even if for hours afterward stray flakes of it do embarrassingly sift off onto the newlyweds in public places, nonetheless, the blushing bride is always admirable, and no one looks at the groom. May we add to the new Mr. and Mrs., wherever they may be, hopefully their future will be as pleasant as the expression that they and Norman Rockwell have left on the chambermaids' faces.

It was during this week that the United States Chamber of Commerce in Washington designated nine persons as great living Americans, and one was *Saturday Evening Post* cover artist Norman Rockwell. His citation read: "Through the magic of your talent, the folks next door—their gentle sorrows, their modest joys—have enriched our own lives and given us a new insight into our countrymen."

SE

The Saturday Evening

POST

June 29, 1957 – 15¢

HERE'S HOW I CHEAT YOU
By a Gyp Furniture Salesman

PARADISE FOR HORSE PLAYERS | BY RED SMITH

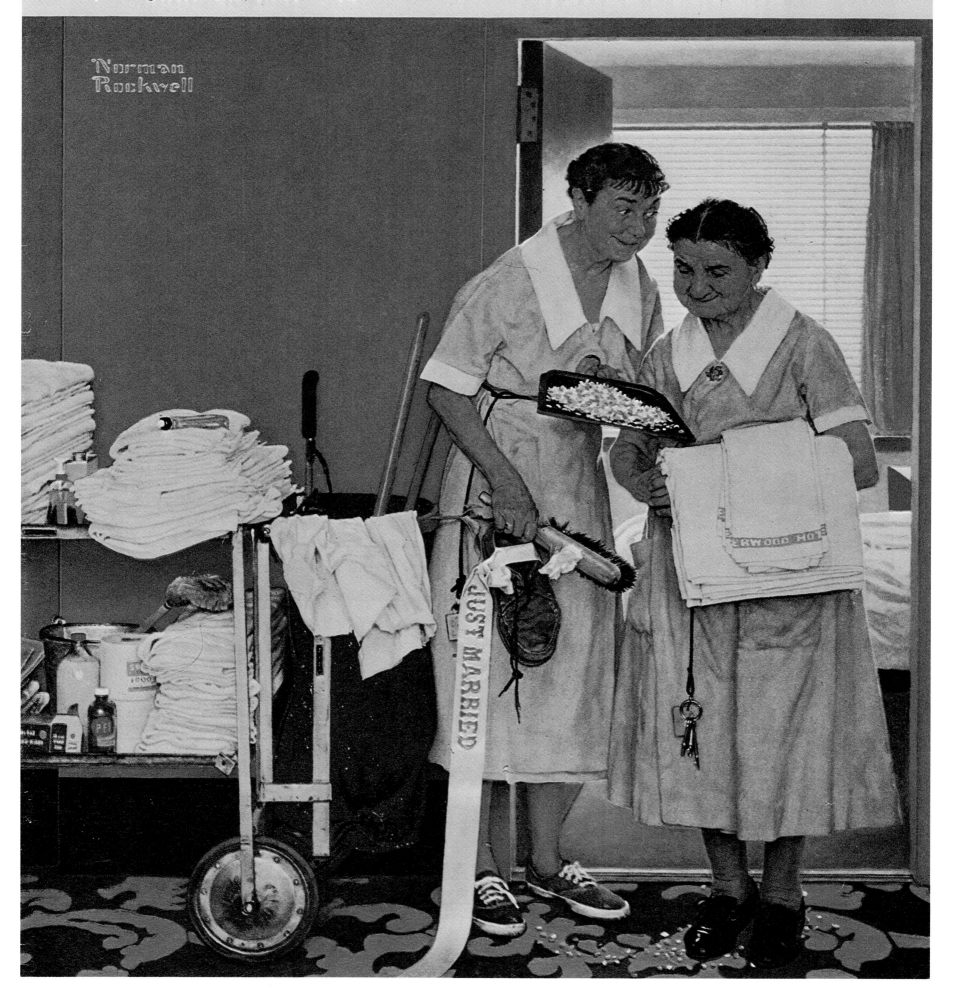

"The Missing Tooth"

In 1957 Norman Rockwell was painting a series of advertisements for Crest toothpaste. "Look, Ma! No cavities!" Norman had asked Anne Morgan, the daughter of friends, to pose for the ads. When she showed up at the studio, she had two front teeth missing. It was a simple matter for the artist to paint in the teeth for the ads, but it set him to thinking. This *Post* cover was the result.

The young lady in the picture, now Anne Morgan Baker, said, "Being on a cover changed my life in one sense of the word. People were always saying 'I saw you in Chicago' or 'I saw you in a drugstore window in New York.' I thought of myself as a tiny, little international star in those days, and $25 when you're six years old is a lot of money." Anne Morgan went on to become a schoolteacher, and the children in her classes were always amused to know that she had been a Rockwell model. One day, a little girl came up to Anne and told her that she had bought a wastebasket with her picture on it. The supreme compliment.

The Saturday Evening

POST

September 7, 1957 ~ *15¢*

PIGSKIN PREVIEW

I Call on Phil Silvers
By PETE MARTIN

Norman Rockwell

"The Expense Account"

The homebound train's wheels efficiently go clickety-clack, but Mr. Hall's brains aren't working quite as well; he has a serious problem with his expense account. Ernest's problem is to be able to state logically where the money went so that his boss won't say he has been spending it like a drunken sailor. Ernest Hall was a friend of Norman Rockwell's in Stockbridge, and because he worked and owned his own taxi company, he could make out his own expense accounts. When Norman couldn't locate the kind of Pullman chair that he wanted, he contacted the Santa Fe Railway. The company graciously sent Rockwell the car chair, which he promptly returned after the picture was completed. Norman nicknamed the fellow with the huge headache "Glad-hand Charlie."

The Saturday Evening POST

November 30, 1957 – 15¢

HAL MARCH'S OWN STORY: The $64,000 and I

From   M. to   M. Total   days

See other side of sheet for instructions

EXPENSE ACCOUNT

Name Ernest Hall

DATE Nov. 22, 1957

Items	D.	11-18	11-19	11-2	11-22	
Rail and A		50.79			5.08	Approved
Sleeping a		1.25			1.25	
Name of Ho		he St. R				
Hotel Expen		16.80				Charge Account
Breakfast						
Lunch		3				2-411-68
Dinner						Total Amount
Street Cars; Taxi,						
Tel. and Tel.					.74	
Entertaining					.60	Signed
Baggage						
Total						

Date				Amount
18.57	*Dinner and en		bridge	70
	C. Segar, Eu			
19.57	Entertainment			65
20.57	Dinner — Mr. + M			40
21.57	*Luncheon and enter	+ McCarthy		
	Miss Charlotte Cavanaugh			$16 35
21.57	Dinner: Frank Sellars, Francis Brennan, D. Schneider			

Norman Rockwell

"Before the Shot"

We see in this all-too-familiar scene the doctor at his instruments table preparing the shot while the young man has partially lowered his pants, preparing the target. Before that rather unpleasant moment when the shot does hit, young Eddie Lock is shown checking out Dr. Donald Campbell's credentials. This particular cover occasioned a great argument among Norman's family and friends as to just how much of the boy's fanny should show. Some said more, some less. Norman finally locked himself in his studio, and after thinking about it for some time, lowered Eddie's pants to their present position—a compromise that avoided shocking nudity and yet revealed enough to provoke humor. Dr. Campbell remembered Norman Rockwell as a kind, generous, thoughtful man who never failed to greet a person on the street with a genuine smile and a hearty "Hello! How are things?"

The Saturday Evening

POST

March 15, 1958 — 15¢

I SHOOT THE BIG SHOTS
By a White House Photographer

We Couldn't Pay Our Bills
By an Installment-Plan Slave

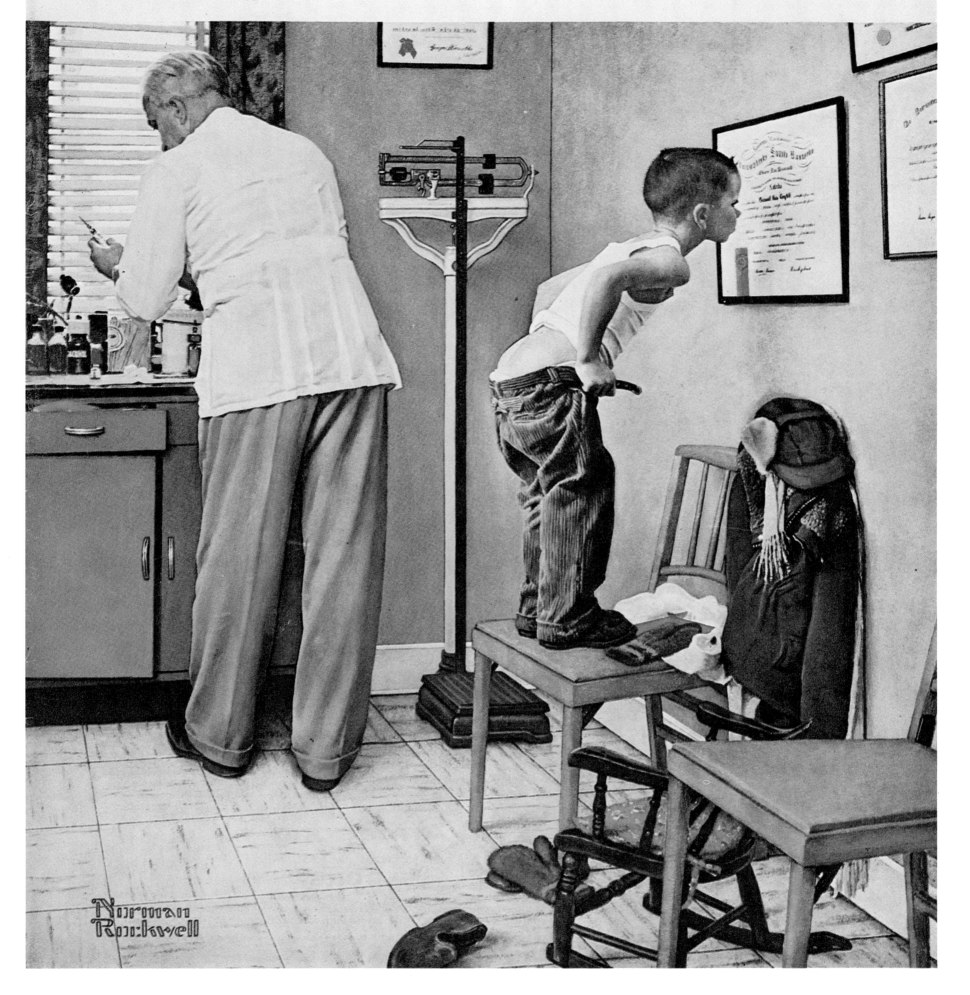

Norman Rockwell

"Weighing In"

This *Post* cover almost led Norman Rockwell off the straight and narrow path. While photographing Eddie Arcaro, who posed for the jockey at Santa Anita Race Track, Norman bet $2 and won $140. He thought perhaps at that time that he would give up painting for betting. He quickly changed his mind, however, after he spent almost the entire $140 buying refreshments for the reporters in the press box who placed the bet for him.

When Norman met Eddie at Santa Anita, he found the jockey to be " . . . a wonderful little guy. My cover, as usual, has some trifle exaggerations, but I'm sure that he won't mind that." Before a jockey goes out to a race, he weighs out. After a race, as you can see, he weighs back in. There are only three basic elements in this picture: the jockey, the track steward, and the scale on which Arcaro is being weighed. Rockwell made much of the contrast in size between Arcaro and the steward. Putting the emphasis on size by having the bigger fellow hunched over as he reads the scale, we get the impression that he would literally tower over the jockey were he to straighten up. Note the bright color of the racing silks, the mud spattered on the white riding pants, the stripes of the steward's shirt, and other details. It is not surprising that when Rockwell accepted the assignment of a racing theme he chose to portray this small, private drama rather than the public spectacle of the actual race.

NW

The Saturday Evening
POST
June 28, 1958 – 15¢

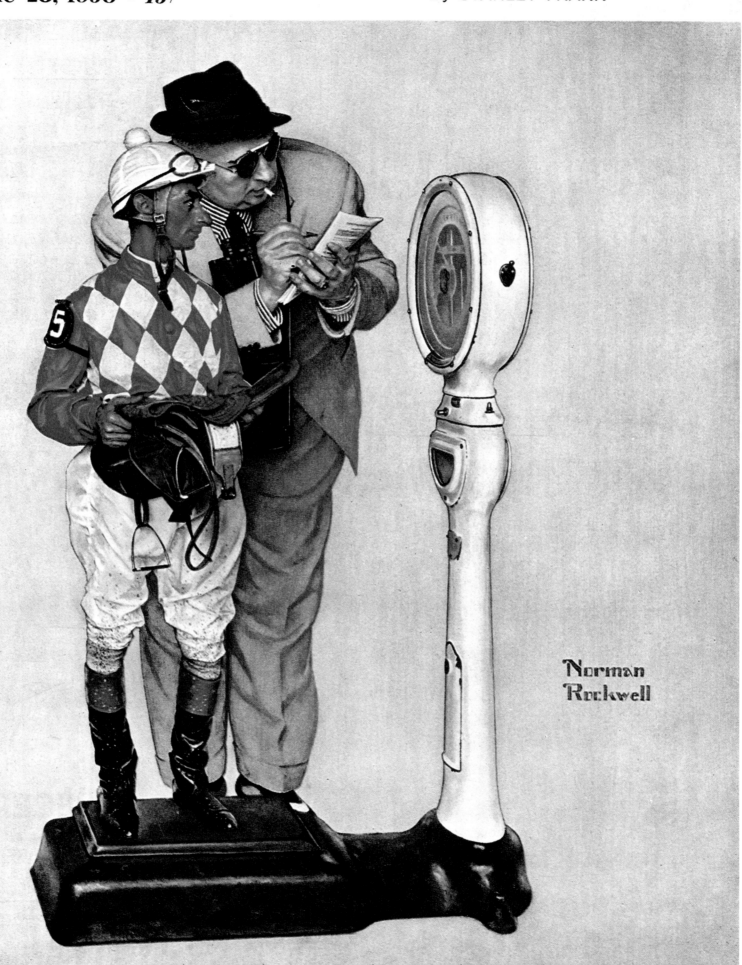

Norman Rockwell

"Knothole Baseball"

How wonderful it would be to be youthful again and to relive the joy of seeing a ball game through a knothole. Most knotholes are made by Mother Nature in her unhurried way. If she were too slow, however, a boy could help her along by removing the knot with his trusty jackknife or by giving it a good swat with a stone. As you no doubt recall, this should be done rather secretly (preferably at night); otherwise the caretaker of the baseball grounds may chase the boy with a stick and then nail a piece of tin over the new hole. A darn mean thing to do! Unlike anyone else, however, Norman Rockwell made his knothole with a paintbrush. Many art experts, seeing not only the knothole itself but the wood around it, felt that Rockwell's treatment of wood looked more realistic than wood itself. One might also note that the ever youthful Norman, rather than signing his name with his usual open-block or script letters, determined that it would be much more fun to carve his name right into the wood.

"The Runaway"

Norman Rockwell painted this, as well as many other covers, twice. He changed the background from an urban Howard Johnson's to a rural lunchroom because he wanted to convey the idea that the kid had gotten well out of town before being apprehended. He used this particular fellow as a model for the counterman because he thought a jaded, worldly type would be more understanding than a young fellow. This picture typifies a line from Frank Sinatra's famous song "The House I Live In" in which he sings of the "big things and the small." It shows the common bond of understanding in friendship that can be present between a large, understanding policeman and a little boy running away from home.

Richard Clemens, a neighbor of Rockwell's, was indeed a Massachusetts State Police officer and was simply delighted when Rockwell called him and asked him to pose for this picture. Clemens said of Rockwell, "His art is timeless. It has proven to be pleasing to people of all ages." The model for the runaway was young Eddie Lock, the same fellow you met in a previous *Post* cover, "Before the Shot." After posing for this picture in 1958, Clemens and Lock did not see each other again until 1971; both were taking a course in logic during evening classes at Berkshire Community College and ended up sitting side by side.

Some of the details you may want to note in this picture are: In 1958, the stools of those counters were spring-loaded; you will notice that the policeman's stool is a bit lower than Eddie's because of his extra weight. Note also that as you look into the chrome of the stools, you can see the reflection of the front of the store behind us. Other things such as Eddie's falling socks, his untidy shoes, the sugar on the counter (still on a bit of an angle), the coffee just turning brown, the counterman just sprouting a new mustache, the menu behind the gentleman, the old-fashioned radio, and the cherry pie, all make for one more Rockwell triumph.

The Saturday Evening POST

September 20, 1958 – *15¢*

Mickey Cohen:
The Private Life of a Hood
By Dean Jennings

"The Losing Candidate"

Candidate Casey has had it. It is all over now, including the shouting. The "people's choice" has not been chosen by the people. It was a hard-fought campaign, and one that Casey was most confident would bring a victory. Once again, though, no one can predetermine the voters' choice.

Rockwell very much enjoyed working with the delightful chap with the cigar in his mouth—Tom Carey—from Stockbridge, Massachusetts. Carey carried the Stockbridge mail from the railroad station via horse and buggy to the post office for fifty years or more. During the summer, he also drove tourists about the countryside in his surrey, pointing out places of interest such as: the Old Mission House, the Indian graveyard, and of course, the Old Corner House, where so many of Norman's originals can be viewed today.

The model for Casey was indeed Bernard T. Casey, a Democrat from Boston. For some years prior to this cover's appearance, Mr. Casey, a telephone company executive, had served eight terms in the State Legislature. He then quit running to concentrate on earning his daily bread, but this natural-born leader with the winning smile never did quit helping other people campaign and win.

The Saturday Evening
POST
November 8, 1958 ~ 15¢

Our Own Inside Story
By Joseph and Stewart Alsop

RALPH BELLAMY:
The Man Who Plays FDR

"The Holdout"

Selecting the right models for any painting is extremely important, as it is up to the artist to tell the story through the characters. One of the reasons that Rockwell preferred to live in a small town rather than in a city was that in a town he knew just about everybody, and just about everybody knew him. There was always a large number of people whose faces Norman was familiar with, and because they all knew Norman, most were willing to pose. As a matter of fact, no one ever refused him.

The characters in this cover are a pretty good cross-section of the people of Stockbridge. There were a couple of ringers, however. The man with the mustache standing beside the sleeping juryman is Bob Brooks, who was an art director in a New York advertising agency. The lady in the man's world is Bob's wife, Barbara. There isn't space here to review the evidence, but judging from the debris on the table and floor, we may assume that the jury has been in session for many hours; a lone female juror is clearly the reason for the length of the deliberation. The lady has firmly made up her mind that, by golly, no one is going to tell her how to vote. "But Ma'am, you're not being logical!" "My dear sir, I know how I feel. Don't I?" Norman Rockwell said that he could not imagine who would win this battle despite the fact that he himself was on the jury. That's Norman in the blue shirt behind the lady trying to be a persuading factor. Norman said that he was there in the picture because he's thrifty—he didn't have to pay himself a model's fee. Louie Lamone, Norman's good friend and confidant, is shown here in a red shirt and jacket. With a cigarette in his mouth, he is listening to everyone else give his side of the argument before jumping in with his own powers of persuasion.

The Saturday Evening

POST

August 27, 1960 – *15¢*

Art Linkletter
TELLS HIS OWN STORY

5TH AV
W 54 ST

norman rockwell

"The Window Washer"

When this cover came out, many Americans began to wonder what had ever come over Norman Rockwell. His last two covers had dealt with shapely young women. Norman once made the statement, "Without shapely young ladies to admire, the only thing left to look at would be flowers and trees." In explaining his use of this attractive young woman, he said, "At first I had a very prim girl looking shocked, but the idea of youth calling to youth worked out more effectively." He continued, "The girl isn't going to date the fellow, however. The public may be assured of that."

All right, this is a business office, so let's get down to the business at hand. J. J. Fuddy of Fuddy, Clamwhistle, and Dovetonsils Associates is dictating a letter, which (if we read the secretary's shorthand correctly) begins as follows: "Gentlemen: I am in receipt of yours of the twenty-first . . ." And if we read her expression correctly, she's thinking, "Men! They're either too fresh or too stuffy!"

The Saturday Evening

POST

September 17, 1960 – 15¢

"John F. Kennedy"

In the summer of 1960, Norman Rockwell received an assignment from the *Post* which he found most interesting. He was told to visit John F. Kennedy, a young and not very well-known senator who had surprised many people by rounding up most of the delegates for the upcoming Democratic convention. Rockwell has to paint a cover featuring him to appear in October of that year.

The Kennedy cover painting was started at the family compound in Hyannisport in June, a month before his nomination. Rockwell arrived at Kennedy's home early June 11 to begin his work. When he rang the doorbell, Kennedy, still in pajamas, called to him to make himself comfortable. "The pajamas were rumpled, but he was wonderful." When the sitting had gotten under way, Kennedy had one request. He asked Rockwell to make him look at least his age. Kennedy, you see, was only 43 at the time, not very old as presidential timber, and with his boyish face, he looked even younger. The senator was extremely friendly, Norman recollected. The sitting was divided into two sessions. After Norman had sketched for about an hour, the pair knocked off long enough to take a bit of a rest. JFK and his guest then strolled down to the ocean, where Kennedy gave him a tour of his boat which was tied up at the dock. Norman remembered, "He was a marvelous host, and very considerate."

This was not the last painting that Rockwell was to do of JFK. He painted him again in 1963. He also painted Kennedy in a Peace Corps picture, which now hangs in the Old Corner House museum in Stockbridge, and had also painted him in a convention scene, "A Time for Greatness."

The Saturday Evening POST

October 29, 1960 — 15¢

WITH CANDIDATE KENNEDY ON CAMPAIGN

HOW TO CATCH A FALLING SPACE CAPSULE

WILL MEXICO TAKE THE "CASTRO" WAY?

EILEEN FARRELL: OFFBEAT PRIMA DONNA

Norman Rockwell

"Richard M. Nixon"

Shortly after Rockwell completed his portrait of Kennedy, he began another portrait of Kennedy's opponent, Richard Nixon. After this initial effort, he made other portraits of Nixon, and in fact, Nixon was the president that he painted the most—a total of six times. Later on, Rockwell observed, "His looks haven't changed so much over the years. Oh, he's older, sure. Aren't we all? But the features strike me as being pretty much the same. Maybe it's that Nixon nose. It's hell to paint and to keep it from dominating too much," he once confided. Later, Rockwell added, "When that Nixon smiled, he was just about as warm and friendly as the father of two pretty daughters could be."

The Saturday Evening
POST

November 5, 1960 — *15¢*

Norman Rockwell

"The Golden Rule"

Generally, for an April painting, Norman would try to think of something gay, light, humorous, and mind-bending. Through his *Post* covers, he felt most of the time that he should try to entertain, but once in a while, he got an uncontrollable urge to be serious. Like everyone else, he was concerned with the world situation, and the only way he felt he could contribute something was through his paintings. So, for quite some time, he tried to think of something that might be of help to the greater part of humanity.

One day (and Rockwell didn't remember when, how, or why) he suddenly got the idea that the "Golden Rule" ("Do unto others as you would have them do unto you") was the subject he was looking for. Right away he got intensely excited. But how should he depict the theme? He began to make all sorts of sketches, but then remembered that down in the cellar of his studio was a 10-foot long, unfinished, charcoal drawing of a United Nations picture. Norman hauled it upstairs. Noting that he had tried to depict all the peoples of the world gathered together, he decided that the theme was exactly what he wanted to express about his "Golden Rule."

Norman spent almost five months and an enormous amount of work while painting this picture, but he never became discouraged nor stopped thinking that the project was worthwhile. The more he painted, the more excited he became.

The one point that pleased Norman the most was that the models, although internationally representative, all came from his hometown area. Though many of the models' costumes (from Norman's own studio wardrobe) were collected from around the world on Rockwell's many trips abroad, the people are all local—either from Stockbridge or from Arlington, Vermont, not far away. Norman chuckled when he declared, "Oh, and the rabbi, he's Mr. Lawless, our retired postmaster. I put whiskers on him, and I think he fits the part quite well even if he is a Catholic." One face in the painting, located in the upper-right hand corner, Norman painted from memory; it was his late wife, Mary, and the baby she is holding is their first grandson, a child she never lived to know.

After "The Golden Rule" appeared as a magazine cover, Norman Rockwell was presented with the Interfaith Award from the National Conference of Christians and Jews, a citation he treasured, because it recognized "his dedication to the highest ideals of amity, understanding, and cooperation among men, and his artistic leadership in depicting with such exacting technique, with unfailing humor, the universal fact that all men, great and unknown, are members of the one family of man under God." What a perfect description of Norman's philosophy of life.

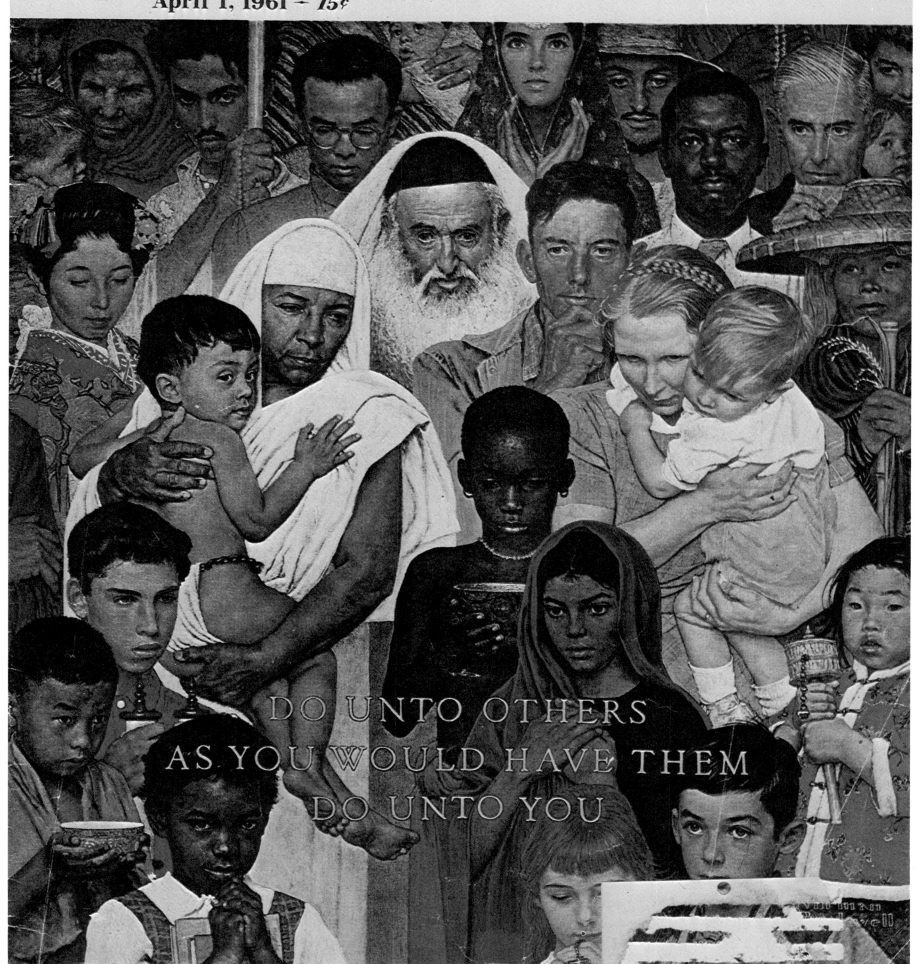

The Saturday Evening
POST
April 1, 1961 – *15¢*

THE **NEW** UTAH

My Adventures Among the U.S. Senators
By DEAN ACHESON

DO UNTO OTHERS
AS YOU WOULD HAVE THEM
DO UNTO YOU

"Modernizing the Post"

In 1728, an enterprising young fellow by the name of Benjamin Franklin began a new publication called "The Universal Instructor in All Arts and Sciences and Pennsylvania Gazette." Keeping in step with the times, *The Saturday Evening Post,* on occasion, changed its appearance and applied new makeup. In this cover, no change in name came about, but the makeup has been brightened considerably. Shown here in the cover is *Post* designer Herbert Lubalin, who has tucked the *Saturday Evening* inside a bigger and perkier *Post*. The artist who painted this picture is that slim young man who first captivated *Post* readers in 1916. Just for fun, Rockwell has altered his signature (employing a modern lettering) for this renascent occasion.

CASEY STENGEL
HIS OWN STORY

PLUS: KENNEDY'S
"REPORT CARD" By STEWART ALSOP

POST
The Saturday Evening

Sept. 16, 1961

20¢

Norman Rockwell

"The Cheerleader"

It is rather fitting that this cover was chosen to appear during Thanksgiving, the height of the football season. Norman, rather obviously, agreed with Maurice Chevalier's statement "Thank heaven for little girls" when he selected this pretty and perky girl.

Norman depicted this mercurial cheerleader swiveling back and forth to watch the action on the field while trying to keep the rooters rooting. In a moment of despair, she misses the split-second shift in the fortunes of her team when Number 10 recovers a fumble. Then the uproar from the stands toward a sure touchdown, leaving the volatile miss to cartwheel in joy. That hair ribbon tells the whole moral of the story: When all looks lost, don't stay tied up in a knot.

PT 109: THE ORDEAL OF KENNEDY AND HIS MEN AS CASTAWAYS UNDER FIRE

SPEAKING OUT: ARE CHILDREN'S BOOKS TRASH?

POST
The Saturday Evening

Nov. 25, 1961

20¢

"The Connoisseur"

At first glance, one would almost assume that Norman Rockwell's intent in this *Post* cover was to make fun of contemporary art, and perhaps this was the case. One is not really sure whether the prosperous-looking art collector examining this Jackson Pollock-like form of art is about to reach for his checkbook to buy the painting or is simply looking at it and saying "What is it?" As Rockwell explained, "If I were young now, I might paint that way myself. Recently I attended some classes in modern art techniques. I learned a lot and loved it." He further added, "I wish I'd had those lessons before I did this cover." He remembered this project as being a lot of fun but not something he'd like to pursue as a steady routine.

The artist did have a great deal of fun painting his abstraction. He simply placed the canvas down on the floor, dipped his brushes into paints, and splashed them all over, far and wide. When he got tired of his dripping paint brush, he invited a man, who was painting the windows of this studio, to help. From the top of his ladder, the fellow obligingly dumped a can of white paint on the canvas spread out on the floor.

THE LITTLE-KNOWN WORLD OF
OUR NEGRO ARISTOCRACY

BACKSTAGE WITH
ACADEMY AWARD WINNER
Shirley Jones

POST
The Saturday Evening

Jan.13,1962

20¢

Norman
Rockwell

"Midnight Snack"

Norman Rockwell would often browse around museums of all types looking for thoughts and ideas he could use in his cover paintings. Some of these ideas which almost came into fruition were: a little old lady looking at a reclining nude with wonder and disdain, a young couple gazing longingly upon a Parisian street scene, or a little boy about to climb upon a marble statue.

Norman claimed that he got the idea for this cover painting after visiting the John Woodman Higgins Armory Museum in Worcester, Massachusetts, where he saw one of the world's finest collections of armor and weapons. The horse and rider are part of the Higgins collection, but the bored guard eating his lunch and the disapproving stare of the horse are strictly out of the famed Rockwell imagination.

The Saturday Evening
POST
November 3, 1962   20¢

Eichmann And His Trial
By His Prosecutor
The Attorney General of Israel

A Short Story by William Saroyan

| **Memoirs of a Monster**
By Boris Karloff | **California Feud**
L.A. vs. S.F. | **'Genius' at Green Bay**
Fullback Jim Taylor |

"Prime Minister Nehru"

In 1962 Norman and Molly took a long trip almost around the world while they met, and he painted, a series of world leaders. Among those leaders was Prime Minister Nehru of India. Molly was not just along for the ride, however. She decided that if Norman was going to be working, she would also. Before they left, she took a crash course in professional photography so that she would be able to shoot pictures to be used as a record of their trip. That education in photography served her well on many trips thereafter.

On November 18, the Rockwells and their traveling companions boarded a plane headed east. About twenty-four hours later, they arrived in New Delhi. A few days later, they were introduced to the prime minister at a small luncheon. Rockwell was invited to Nehru's office, where he made some sketches. Most of the painting of the finished portrait was done in a hotel room and about two weeks after he began, the finished oil was shipped to the United States.

When Rockwell first met Nehru, he was wearing a dark suit. When he went to sketch him the next day, Nehru again had dark clothing on. So, Norman asked him if he wouldn't please put on a white outfit and cap, to which Nehru replied he never wore white that season of the year (during the cooler months). Norman explained to him, however, that the American people who would see his picture in a magazine would imagine that he always wore white, tight suits like a maharaja. Nehru chuckled and said, "If that's what they expect, that's what we'll give them." He then went out of the room and came back in the all-white outfit you see now on the cover. Norman explained, "He certainly was most accommodating." Norman and Molly liked India very much, and they were invited to Nehru's home, where they chatted with his daughter, Indira Gandhi. The Rockwells were amazed and flattered to find that Madame Gandhi had a room lined with prints of Rockwell's paintings for her children.

POST

THE SATURDAY EVENING POST JANUARY 19 • 1963 20c

NEHRU
His Crisis with China
Exclusive Interview
By ROBERT SHERROD

Fiction by Graham Greene, William Saroyan, Joan Williams

Norman Rockwell
New Delhi, India

Air Crashes A growing peril • **TEDDY & TAFT** Go to Washington

"Well!!"

Norman Rockwell flew to Los Angeles to do the cover portrait of Jack Benny. When he arrived there, this man, who had painted some of the world's most famous faces, anxiously telephoned the *Post*'s Bill Davidson. "Bill," he said, "I'm really nervous about meeting this Benny fellow. Would you be good enough to help me over the hurdle of meeting Jack Benny." Davidson was glad to comply, for half an hour earlier, Jack Benny, the shy friend of presidents, kings, and queens, had phoned Davidson and asked him to be on hand when it came time for him to meet Rockwell. Benny was just as nervous. Yes, Jack Benny was the man who misered his way into America's heart, who never grew older than his 39 years, whose folded arms and sideward glance always suggested an answer to the question "Your money or your life," and who replied, "I'm thinking, I'm thinking!" Rockwell said later that he was really tempted to ask Benny if he actually kept his money in a basement vault.

POST

THE SATURDAY EVENING POST MARCH 2 • 1963 20c

"Life begins at 39"

JACK BENNY

Back on Broadway after 32 years

Fiction by JOHN O'HARA

Norman Rockwell

"Worried President"

In this Kennedy portrait, the second published by the *Post,* Norman Rockwell captured the President in a pensive moment, his face showing the great burden of his executive position. In a March 1963 press conference, John F. Kennedy remarked, "If you ask me if this was the winter of our discontent, I would say no. If you would ask me if we were quite as well this winter as perhaps we were doing in the fall, I might say no."

The nation noticed a remarkable contrast between the fall 1962 Kennedy and the winter 1963 Kennedy. After the President's famous confrontation, when he forced Nikita Khrushchev to back off, Kennedy was riding high. Soon, however, more troubles began to emerge: troubles with Canada, turmoil in the Middle East, high unemployment. Events in the Far East were going badly. The Kennedy tax program bogged down on Capitol Hill. Difficulties arose with Cuba and Charles de Gaulle. Kennedy's grand design was going down the tubes. We knew it, the nation knew it, and Norman Rockwell knew it.

Norman captured the feeling, the pain and agony, of the President. He felt a special kinship with Kennedy, not only for the fact that they were both from the same state, but for the fact that Rockwell had spent some time with Kennedy and felt him to be a friend. There was a touch of sadness in Rockwell's voice as he once remarked, "With all of the troubles he's having, I really wish there were some way that I could help that young fellow."

POST

THE SATURDAY EVENING POST APRIL 6 · 1963 20c

Easter Bonnets
The mad hatters who make them .

Canadian Elections
Will anti-Americanism triumph?

A WORRIED PRESIDENT:

THE CRISIS IN HIS FOREIGN POLICY

BY STEWART ALSOP

PAINTING BY NORMAN ROCKWELL

THE BOXING MESS by ex-promoter Bill Fugazy / **DOROTHY LOUDON** the new Carol Burnett

"Gamal Abdel Nasser"

On the same trip that the Rockwells took to India, they also went to Egypt. There, Norman encountered some difficulty in working with the Egyptian president. He was a rather handsome man and was very conscious of the fact. "When I tried to paint him," Norman said, "he kept giving me that big, 'Hello, folks!' smile." Norman felt that the straight-on view would show too much teeth, and he didn't want that. Nasser understood perfectly what Rockwell wanted, since the president spoke beautiful English. He insisted, however, that he was going to have things his way. Norman kept insisting on a profile, Nasser kept insisting on a frontal view. Finally, in spite of the big, tough guards that were all over the place, Norman took Nasser by the shoulder and just moved him around the way he wanted him to stand. He then began to sketch. Nasser immediately turned around and came out with that big toothpaste smile again. Norman had to push him around once more, and finally Nasser gave in. Rockwell recalled, "He was a tough one, though. Looked the part of a revolutionary. Quite a tall man, with a proud, straight bearing. I thought he looked like a handsome headwaiter."

POST

THE SATURDAY EVENING POST MAY 25 · 1963 20c

In defense of women
by Taylor Caldwell

Los Angeles' Mayor Yorty

Nasser's turbulent world
an exclusive interview
by ROBERT SHERROD

Norman Rockwell

Cairo, U.A.R.

Zermatt's shame legacy of a typhoid epidemic / **Turbine auto** resurgent Chrysler takes a gamble

"John F. Kennedy: In Memoriam"

This cover painting by Norman Rockwell was greatly admired by the late President Kennedy. It first appeared on October 29, 1960, and was republished by the *Post* on December 14, 1963, as the memorial tribute to him. Norman Rockwell was so distressed about the assassination of John Kennedy, his friend and his President, that he determined that this would be his last cover for *The Saturday Evening Post*. This move ended a 47-year career and the love affair between a giant publishing firm and a giant of a man.

On May 23, 1976, the citizens of Stockbridge held a celebration in honor of Norman Rockwell. With great delight, Norman sat and watched a two-hour parade, barbershop quartets, high school bands, Girl and Boy Scout honor guards. After this exciting and exhausting day, reporters asked Norman how he felt. His reply, as usual, was brief. "I'm tired, but proud."

POST

THE SATURDAY EVENING POST DECEMBER 14 • 1963 20c

IN MEMORIAM
A senseless tragedy

THE NEW PRESIDENT

JOHN F. KENNEDY
1917-63

"A Visit with Norman Rockwell"

With the rejuvenation of *The Saturday Evening Post,* it was fitting that a picture of Norman Rockwell appeared on the cover. So, it was appropriate when the time came in 1971 to create the cover of the summer 1971 edition of *The Saturday Evening Post* that the mountain should move at last to Mohammed, and the editors of the magazine should journey to honor the man who, in his lifetime, had come to personify the magazine, and to work with him in the comfort of his classic home and studio in Stockbridge, high in the Berkshire hills of western Massachusetts.

And it was also fitting that on the newest of Rockwellian covers a small boy appeared, complete with red hair, freckles, and a missing tooth, the true mixture of all the typical little boys that preceded him over the years, part angel, part devil. And so the editors found such a boy in Indianapolis, Indiana, the new home of the Curtis Publishing Company and took him with them to unite this symbol of young America with septuagenarian-artist who had already sketched hundreds of such small boys, each uniquely himself and still all boys in one. The boy's name was Brian and the artist dressed him in the garb of the early *Saturday Evening Post* delivery boys. He was seven years old and had trepidations about meeting one of the most famous 77-year-old men in the world, but the minute the two met, all such fears vanished.

IND

THE SATURDAY EVENING POST

Founded A ... by Benj. Franklin

Summer 1971   One Dollar

Norman Rockwell, born in 1894 in New York City, is probably the most popular American artist and illustrator of the twentieth century. His paintings, capturing everyday people in everyday situations, are a pictorial history of our nation—and few, if any of us, cannot relate to the stories they tell.

Rockwell studied at the Chase School of Art, the National Academy of Art, and the Art Students League. He later served as an active member of the faculty of the Famous Artists School in Westport, Connecticut.

His work first appeared in *Boy's Life, St. Nicholas, American Boy, Country Gentleman,* and other magazines, as well as in books for children. Much of his talent has been devoted to painting for the Boy Scouts of America's renowned calendar series, and he has illustrated many of the Scout's handbooks.

Rockwell gained great popularity as a cover illustrator for *The Saturday Evening Post* and other magazines, developing a style of finely drawn, clear realism with a wealth of anecdotal detail. He also did art work for many major advertisers. Among the many advertisements Rockwell accepted a commission to do, one of his largest and finest undertakings was a series of over seventy pencil sketches depicting the American Family and the American way of life. These sketches were incorporated into advertisements for a major insurance company.

Rockwell's series on the "Four Freedoms" of the Atlantic Charter was widely circulated during the second World War and even today is numbered among the all-time classics. He gained additional recognition with his moonshot paintings, now in the Smithsonian Institution. He is represented in the Metropolitan Museum of Art, and was named "Artist of the Year, 1969" by his colleagues of the Artists Guild of New York.

Following his early years in New York, Rockwell moved to Arlington, Vermont. In 1943 a fire in his studio in Arlington destroyed many of his original paintings and over the years many other Rockwell paintings have simply disappeared. Included among those no longer accounted for were many of the original paintings prepared for *Saturday Evening Post* covers. Many of the original covers have disappeared, and those that remain have become rare collectors items.

No one captured America like Rockwell. "I paint life as I would like it to be," he once said. "If there was a sadness in this creative world of mine, it was a pleasant sadness. If there were problems, they were humorous problems. I'd rather not paint the agonizing crises and tangles of life."

Norman Rockwell is gone. He died on November 8, 1978, and was laid to rest beneath a brilliant, sunlit November sky on Veterans Day 1978, surrounded by his family and friends and an honor guard of his beloved Boy Scouts. It was a scene worthy of one of his paintings, and perhaps somewhere up there, Norman was busily sketching, hoping to beat the deadline of eternity.